girl...

The Edmonton Queen

next time,
we'll teach you to
walk in heels !!!

♡ Gloria
+
Darrin

THE Edmonton Queen*

*Not a Riverboat Story

Darrin Hagen

Slipstream Books

The Edmonton Queen: not a riverboat story

A Slipstream book
from River Books, an imprint of the Books Collective

River Books and the Books Collective acknowledge the support of the Alberta Foundation for the Arts for its grants to publishers.
We acknowledge the support of the Canada Council for the Arts for our publishing programme.

Editor for the press: Candas Jane Dorsey Outside editor: Timothy J. Anderson
Front cover photograph copyright ©1993 by Peter McClure.
Cover design by Vern Busby, Totino Busby Design.
Inside photo credits, see p. 164. Every effort has been made to locate the copyright holders of the photographs contained herein. If you took one of these photographs and were not credited, please get in touch with the publisher at the address below and you will receive credit in a future edition.

Inside design and page set-up by Ike at the Wooden Door, in Flange Light and Ann (True-Type Fonts) in Word for Windows 6. Printed at Priority Printing, Edmonton, on 50lb. Offset White with covers of Cornwall Cover.
Thanks to Kim Smith at Priority Printing.

Published in Canada by Slipstream (River) Books, an imprint of the Books Collective, 214-21, 10405 Jasper Avenue, Edmonton, Alberta, Canada T5J 3S2. Telephone (403) 448 0590.

2 4 6 8 10 9 7 5 3 1

Canadian Cataloguing in Publication Data

Hagen, Darrin, 1964–
The Edmonton queen

ISBN 1-895836-46-8

1. Hagen, Darrin, 1964– 2. Transvestites--Alberta--Edmonton--Biography. 3. Female impersonators--Alberta--Edmonton--Biography. I. Title.
HQ77.H33 1997   306.77   C97-910607-9

THE EDMONTON QUEEN: *NOT A RIVERBOAT STORY*
TABLE OF CONTENTS

Lulu, 1983

For Lulu...

Sometime in every lifetime, you meet a person who changes your perception.

This story is dedicated to the queens who lived it, but none of it would have happened quite the way it did were it not for the boundless enthusiasm, unlimited imagination, and frightening creative streak of Charles Gillis.

Through his eyes the world was a much more intense experience, and my world became a richer, more exciting place.

These stories are his as much as mine; the mythologies sprang from his brow in a Niagara-like torrent as the rest of us struggled to keep up. The Family he created was one we all desperately needed, and one by which we were all nourished. Lonely, shy young men from all over Canada found a way to belong; under his wing, we discovered our worth.

We discovered ourselves.

The language, terminology, humor and mythology that make up this book were authored not by one person, but by many who, through an accident of geography, shared one experience.

All I had to do was remember it.

Like I could forget.

...with love,
Gloria
1997

"HERE I AM.
IN EDMONTON, ALBERTA.
WHAT A DUMP!"
Christopher Peterson impersonating Shirley Maclean
channeling Bette Davis
on JuJu Dogface's Psychic Alliance
"TVTV: Transvestite Television"
Guys in Disguise, Fringe Festival 1995

Gloria, 1993

Gloria

11:30 p.m.
New Year's Eve 1993
downtown Edmonton

Gloria comes offstage panting. She struts on her seven inch stilettos into the dressing room, tosses her jewelry onto the counter and heaves her seven-foot frame into a chair in front of the mirror. Her eyes lock with the reflection of her eyes, heavy and dark, oversize lashes dragging the lids down like a pair of cement pumps. Someone told her once they looked sultry.

She had believed them.

The hair is a giant puff of blond tendrils, piled yet falling, done yet undone. Wide enough on the sides to draw attention away from her so-square shoulders. Ruby plum lips. Beauty mark always here. It's the last thing on and usually the first thing off. But she's not done for the night, so it stays.

Two performances have taken their toll on her makeup. The sweat runs through her eyebrows, collecting in an oil slick under her eyes.

It's the closest she's ever come to looking like a football player.

She crosses her legs and surveys the damage. Phyllis Diller would have an easier job.

She pulls a breast out of her bra and pats her forehead dry. The pancake peels off like cheap paint, forcing her real skin out of hiding. She wails in despair. Fixing a face can take longer than building one from scratch.

And it's only twenty minutes until . . .

Fame. Adulation. The gig of the century.

If someone phoned you and asked if you wanted to go-go dance at the base of the city hall clock tower with a spotlight creating a shadow of your gyrating frame four stories high on New Year's Eve at the stroke of midnight in front of 100,000 people–

You wouldn't consider whether or not it was a good idea to be outside in go-go wear in a minus-40-not-including-wind-chill climate;

You wouldn't consider whether or not it was a good idea to be dressed like that at an alcohol-free-family-food-fun-fireworks-type spectacle;

You would say yes. Immediately. Gloria did.

And now she's faced with emergency facial maintenance, a costume change, packing up her clothes and costumes and transporting them from the Library Theatre across Sir Winston Churchill Square to City Hall at twenty minutes to midnight through tens of thousands of people. In the winter. In heels. Without an assistant.

Gloria was never big on logistics.

Praying silently, she panic powders. A white haze expands around her head as she puffs copious amounts of talcum. Soon she is as pale as Glenn Close in *Dangerous Liaisons*. And just as bitchy. But the black keeps bleeding through like a haunted paint job in a B-movie.

Okay, Don't panic. Plan B.

When all else fails, cover up.

Take out all the pins in the wig. Pull the hair around the face. Tell people you saw it in *Vogue*. Necessity is the dragmother of fashion intervention.

Gloria slips out of her universal "little black dress".*(Author's note; this term is not a literal but a figurative one. A little black dress on Gloria could contain enough fabric to slipcover a hearse. It's all a matter of perspective.)*

She pulls out her one-piece Star Trek jumpsuit with the Tit-to-Toe red stripe down the side, chosen because at least most of her skin will be covered, albeit in some bargain synthetic. She quickly inflates two medium sized balloons, leaving lipstick all over the mouthpieces, and places them in their appropriate position, where they are held in place though the miracle of stretch poly blends.

Then, in horror, her eyes travel down her front where she sees...

The Bulge.

The bane of every queen's existence. The ultimate giveaway. The line separating the men from the broads. The equipment. The boy toy.

In her haste, Gloria had forgotten to pack her dance belt.

The Star Trek Jumpsuit with the Tit-to-Toe red stripe is, in a word, form fitting. It greedily hugs every square millimeter of Gloria's larger-than-life frame. Hardly appropriate for a family gathering. You couldn't even get away with that at a fag bar. Now, without going into gory detail about what a queen does with the equipment while in drag, understand that it can be extremely distracting.

Gloria begins throwing clothes around the room, searching frantically for any solution–a wrap, a scarf, a belt. Nothing. Then her eyes land on the blue feather boa.

Tonight's obviously going to be about improvising.

The boa, wrapped around her hips at crotch level, looks ridiculous. She's beginning to resemble a sci-fi ostrich. But there's just not enough time to come up with anything else.

Outside, on street level, the square is in full winter bloom. Lights. Music. People. Colour. Costumes. Presiding over the whole thing is the city hall clock tower. It reads 11:45.

Gloria has now packed up everything into a frenzy of 7-11 bags, hangers and a battered hockey bag. She has made a decision that the fastest way to city hall is underground. Through the subway tunnel. She bursts into the tunnel, then regrets it immediately as the door safety locks behind her.

The tunnel is harshly lit, throbbing with noise and packed with people as far as you can see. It's the pre-midnight buzz– anticipation and bliss and relief and nostalgia all supercharged with an annual intensity. Children in tinsel masks, adults with balloon helmets, all heading to the fireworks.

Gloria endures the snickers, sneers, the "O my God"s, the kids' rude questions as she tries to jog through the insanity, her heels clicking loudly on the tile, inflated breasts bouncing, the boa around her bottom emphasizing the graceless gait of a giant. Sparks fly on every second step from the missing cap on her right spike; she comes on like some obscene cartoon super heroine on her way to save the planet.

With only minutes remaining.

It's the longest block in her lifetime.

Finally, she arrives at her post. She looks up and her jaw drops.

Somehow, in her head, she had always pictured a gilded go-go cage to cavort in.

Somehow, in her head, she had imagined being surrounded by people delighted at her antics and cheering her on.

Somehow, in her head, she had always pictured it looking more like an episode of Solid Gold.

What she had not imagined was a makeshift plywood platform four feet square, shaky, with nine rickety steps hastily nailed together. Hundreds of yards from the action in the center of the square.

Life can be so cruel.

The clock tower reads 11:51.

Unsteady, she climbs the steps to her post. The platform is small, wobbly and covered in a thin sheet of glare ice. No railing. She turns and sees her silhouette–gigantic, shivering, unsteady, with bad poodle-type hair that moves in the wind like a nest of snakes.

The cold starts to sink in. She begins to dance just to keep warm, but there's not a lot she can manage on the tiny platform. And there's another problem: in minus-forty weather, balloons tend to shrink. Now, the balloons stay in place in the jumpsuit as long as they are large. But the compressed cold air means a difference of about ten bra sizes. Now they shift around as if they're being driven by a remote control in the hands of an insane driving instructor.

Hardly the look she was striving for.

Wearying of her humungous shadow, she turns to look at the square, and that's when it happens.

She stares directly into the million-watt searchlight.

Everything else disappears. Her retinas singe and sizzle, and immediately, temporary blindness sets in. She takes a step too far back and plunges out of sight with a short surprised scream and lands in a crumpled heap in a snow bank.

The clock tower says 11:54. She had danced for exactly three minutes.

Now she limps with one broken high heel, bags in tow, like a crazy bag lady caught in a parade, struggling through the crowd. One breast has wiggled its way toward her shoulder, while its partner has slipped to belt level. Frost has formed on her sultry lashes, making blinking a stiff, crunchy affair. Slipping and lurching, she makes her way through the alley, only to find herself stuck in a dead end. Of course, everything's locked. She can't get through.

The clock tower says 11:59.

The countdown.

At the stroke of midnight, with fireworks going off and people hugging and singing a block away, Gloria falls to her knees and starts to cry. A balloon pops and it starts to snow.

The Gospel According To
The Hole Family

(The Big Onion Chapter)

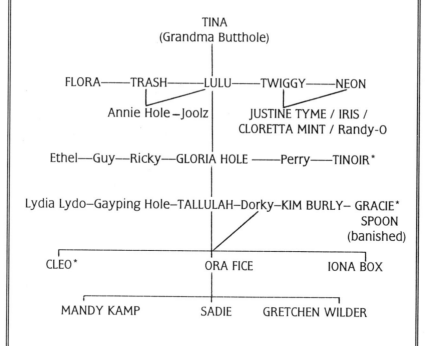

TINA
(Grandma Butthole)

FLORA——TRASH———LULU———TWIGGY———NEON

Annie Hole–Joolz   JUSTINE TYME / IRIS /
                          CLORETTA MINT / Randy-O

Ethel—Guy—Ricky—GLORIA HOLE ——Perry——TINOIR*

Lydia Lydo–Gayping Hole–TALLULAH–Dorky–KIM BURLY– GRACIE*
                                            SPOON
                                            (banished)

CLEO*   ORA FICE   IONA BOX

MANDY KAMP   SADIE   GRETCHEN WILDER

(CAPITALS denote QUEENS, other names are our friends,
* denotes foster children)

Somewhere in a field near Tofield,
sometime near the end of the twentieth century,
on a farm far, far away...

...there may still stand an abandoned outhouse, white paint peeling, door flapping in the wind, the wooden seats long deprived of the touch of moons.

If it still stood, which it may, you could look inside, and it would take a moment to realize that the tiny marks covering the wall are not bugs or dirt but, in fact, writing; dense, confusing writing in Jiffy marker covering all three walls and the inside of the door.

If you could find the beginning of the saga, it would tell you...

First there was Dorkness, then there was Light.
Then there was Bud Light...

You would read on to learn of the creation of Bimbolimbus Slug Destruction, conceived in a flash of cosmic coincidence, who spawned a zillion stars.

Of course, it's all in code.

But a translator could show you that it is, in fact, ancient proof that a mighty family was born in these wilds. The outhouse walls speak as loudly and eloquently as any Rosetta Stone, preserving forever the moment near the end of the millennium when lunacy met inspiration and gave life to a new spirit.

Thus a family was born.

Or at least that's one theory.

Cutting edge grad drag (notice how you just have to
rearrange the letters?), Rocky Mountain House, 1982
Two weeks before I left home.
"Dreams Never Die" was the grad theme.

A River Runs Through It
July, 1982

"You can be whatever you want to be in this life.
Don't ever miss a chance to change the world."
—My Mom

The Greyhound bus leaves Rocky Mountain House twice a day: 7:00 am and suppertime. Not being a morning person, my ticket was for the latter. That way I could say good-bye to Mom, pack my clothes and my accordion, and go watch the North Saskatchewan for a while.

When you stand on a bridge, an illusion occurs. Watching the water slide silently past you in July, the first thing that occurs to you is how clean the water is. A brilliant aquamarine blue that I've never seen anywhere else. The water flowing underneath makes it feel like the whole bridge is moving backward. Suddenly I'm Barbra Streisand on the boat in "Funny Girl" holding that impossible long note.

In Rocky Mountain House you don't tell people you listen to Barbra Streisand.

I took my journal, some school papers, and the love letter from an older man in Edmonton that almost got me thrown out of the house.

An older man. He was 33 then. I'm 33 now. I'm hardly an older man.

I stood on the bridge, ripped them to pieces, and watched them spin and flutter down to the water, where they gradually disappeared into the brilliant clear blue.

I wondered how long it would take to float to Edmonton. If

only I had a boat. I knew where I would end up. I had already been there once.

Flashback.

This is not a riverboat story. It's my story. Actually, it's their story. It's our story.

The Lucky Ones.

The Greyhound stops at Alhambra, Leslieville, Benalto, Eckville, Sylvan Lake and Red Deer.

Keegstra Country.[1]

I could have gotten there faster on the river. I could have *floated* into town.

But back then I was a little more subtle.

At Red Deer, Calgary and Edmonton are exactly the same distance away. Why north? Would things be different if I had turned South?

Probably not. Besides, the river runs north.

And it's my river.

Flashback.

Every once in a while, a queen is born. Whether through osmosis or immaculate misconception is still mostly a mystery, but they appear. Suddenly and without warning, a new pretender to the throne stands in front of you. Under the terms of the Sisterhood of Unrecognized Royalty, they all get their grab at the tiara at some point in their career.

But where do they come from? Genderfuck meteors flaming to earth? Crossdressers crawling from every crevice in the country? Often, they mutate out of men from the most macho of environments. But what triggers it?

For many, the transition is as swift as it is brutal and final. And it happens once a year.

A night where nothing is really what it seems, when pretty boys become susceptible to suggestion, when reality moves aside and dreams take over, when vision is diluted by bright lights, acid trips and masks.

---

[1] Jim Keegstra, a high school teacher in Eckville, was charged with teaching his students that the Holocaust never actually happened. The case recieved national coverage. Eckville is just north of Caroline, where the Aryan Nations have a lovely farm.

Every year, on October 31, thousands of Alberta men cross the line on the one night when they are actually permitted to do so. They cross the line that was drawn in the sandbox in front of them at the age of two. The line that shapes their thinking, their manner, their insecurities, their stress, their careers, their lives, their perception.

They cross that line and for one night, they know.

They put on a dress.

And every year, some of these men don't return.

Because once they're on the other side, the world looks different. And they get hooked. Big time.

The drug of attention, adoration, disgust, applause, glamour, ego, applause, political incorrectness, applause, applause, applause, did I mention applause?

Whether it's because the real world is so drab and hopeless, or because there are too many shackles, or because somebody said "no" one too many times, or because you're too femme to fit, or because it makes your cock hard, or just because you're too fabulously dramatic and stylish for your own good,

You try it.

You love it.

You buy it.

Not just the outfit. The lifestyle.

Gloria, 1987

There is a moment of illumination that very first time, when you finish painting the face. You reach for the wig, slip it on, and your eyes lock with your eyes in the mirror.

For a moment, everything else disappears.

You see someone looking back, a total stranger that you recognize immediately.

You see your sister, your alter ego, the only woman that will ever understand you. A combination of your mother, the wife you'll never have, the woman you'll never be.

Your eyes lock with your eyes, and a destiny you never pictured locks into place.

You fall in love.

With the woman in you.

And the man you thought you were will do anything to make her dreams come true.

It can happen to anyone.

Neon, Gloria, Iris and Lulu, Marilyn night1987
These tiny gowns...the Marilyn gown was worn by Bianca Bang-Bang in the first drag show I ever saw (see photo p. 36).The gown first belonged to Millie, and is still handed down through the Marilyns–Twiggy has it now

These stories are true. Mostly.

The really bizarre stuff is true.

Actually it's *all* true. All I had to do was remember.

Like I could forget.

DARRIN HAGEN

None of the names have been changed, because there are no innocents, but occasionally the outfits I describe are nicer than what we were actually wearing.

It's beyond difficult putting these times and people into perspective. Back then, we had no perspective. The drugs were cheap, and we were beautiful. Or was that the other way around?

There was only the next show, the next party, the next hit, the next john, the next pageant, the next Barbra Streisand album.

The eighties sashayed past us in a crinoline haze, a cloud of dreaming bigger than anyone should. Foam and fur and feathers and false lashes. It was like living backstage with the Muppets, only they were more realistic.

Delusions of Grandeur dressed by Value Village.

Our enormous visions. These tiny gowns.

Lulu, 1983

DARRIN HAGEN

Lulu
sometime in 1982
the Strip: Downtown Edmonton

"Let my life be anything. Anything but boring."
—Lulu LaRude

Lulu stands on the corner of boredom and desperation, her fried Diana Ross wig illuminated by the blinking hotel lights. Pink Yellow Pink Yellow Pink.

Big girl. Built like a Soviet hockey player, but with better fashion sense.

She stands there: All Mood, All Rude, All Attitude.

The cars circle round and round the square, the headlights tracing a thick bright circle around her and she bends down to look in the windows and some cars slow down and some speed up and each get a wink or a finger and some come round again and some give up. But not the Caddy.

Ahhh, the Caddy. Built for comfort. Like her. Lots of leg room. She's a big girl. And she's in heels. And has been for hours.

The Caddy. If she could get in she could rest her size 14B puppies. Her blisters yelp as she struts the sidewalk pretending it doesn't hurt, but it does and she leans on the parking meter and wishes she worked at a Mr. Submarine. They make you wear a hair net, but you get to wear flats.

Ahh, the Caddy. Maximum headroom. Good for big hair. She's a big girl. She wears big hair well.

The Caddy circles like a silver shark, testing the water for motion. Lulu sucks in her waist to appear more willowy. She drags on her Camel, bends down and gives him a look that says, among other things, that if he slammed on his brakes right here, right now, she would be his bendover babydoll for the night. It's a look dripping with enough innuendo to fuel every car that didn't pick her up tonight. That's a lot of juice.

The window opens a crack. Through it she can smell the bucks. Lulu can smell a rich Daddy better than a sow hunting for truffles. It's a heady combo of cigar smoke, anticipation and tinny top forty that envelopes her senses. In his glasses she can see the reflected tail lights of cruising station wagons, sedans on the hunt.

From where he sits, the split ends of her fried Diana Ross wig look like a halo flashing Pink Yellow Pink Yellow Pink.

From where he sits, the safety pins don't show, and the rise and fall of her balloons as she sucks on her Camel make him whimper under his breath.

From where he sits, she's a goddess, floating in a diaphanous fog of exhaust and steam and smoke, swooping down to his car, a heavenly vision of sexual release, an Angel all in black.

He's been drinking.

He looks out the window, sees a sweet young thing. Humpin' on the parking meter, leanin' on the parking meter, oh she looks so good.

The Caddy swims up to the curb. Lulu steps up to the Caddy. The parking meter heaves a sigh of relief. She leans over and coos through the crack, "Wanna play, Daddy?"

As she waits, she shifts the pain in her feet from left to right to left. Anticipation mounts. At this point in her workday, she would suck him off for free just to be able to sit down for ten minutes.

The door clicks open. Lulu folds herself into the passenger seat with the grace of a pro, hair not even touching the roof. She slips off her pumps and rubs her toes together in the heat.

"Seventy bucks and it's yours, Daddy."

But Daddy's not listening. His eyes are glued to her feet. He watches the toes wiggle around under the sheer mesh of four pairs of Shoppers Drug Mart pantyhose. He's wondering if she'll think he's a total pervo because all he really wants is those toes in his mouth.

Lulu sees Daddy eyeing her feet and panic punches her stomach around, because her feet are always a dead giveaway–and this makes her nervous 'cause oddly enough some men get turned off by finding a penis on the woman they're renting–so to change the subject she says,

"You can't fuck me tonight cause I'm on the rag, but I give a blowjob that'll make your head cave in."

As he pulls the Caddy back into the stream of headlights he purrs "How about a foot massage?"

Lulu can't believe her bead encrusted ears. The big hair goddesses were beaming love on her tonight!

They pull into a parking lot littered with used condoms and spent fantasies. Money changes hands, her feet land in his lap and in seconds she's transported into reflexology heaven. He's good.

She moans and gasps, not because that's what she does but because that's what she gets paid to do.

From where he sits, the stubble growing through her thick pancake makeup is merely a halo kissing her cheek.

From where he sits, the oversize special edition lashes, one of which went on a little crooked, are light and wispy like feathers.

From where he sits, the one gradually deflating breast merely adds an asymmetrical loveliness.

He's drunker than he thought.

Suddenly, the night is alive with red and blue and searchlight white and it's a bust, and Lulu freaks because of that silly repeat offender thingy and she makes a break for it.

She falls out of the car and runs for her life, crashing through the underbrush like a bull moose bellowing for freedom. The official insults hurled at her merely bounce off her back. She hits the sidewalk and runs like a girl down the street, arms pumping, purse swinging viciously, balloons heaving from the effort. The Diana Ross wig flies off her head and lands under the wheels of a passing garbage truck. She glances over her shoulder pad to find–no one in pursuit. Running like a girl slows to walking like one. She's free.

And her feet feel fabulous. Daddy knew his stuff.

It is then that she looks down and realizes her size 14B black patent leather come fuck me pumps with Joan Crawford ankle straps are still in the Caddy, with Daddy.

She made seventy bucks. New shoes are $97.50

Back at the Caddy, the cops deal with the john.

The only clue to the girl that got away is a pair of 14B black patent leather come fuck me pumps with Joan Crawford ankle straps. Somewhere out there is a hooker big enough to fill those shoes.

There's a reward. Enough to by a lot of shoes. But she's too embarrassed to collect.

The next night, she's back on her corner.

Lulu going out

DARRIN HAGEN

Flashback
(Not the Literary Device)
1976-1990

"This place can't be real. The boys are prettier than I am!"
—some straight chick who wandered into Flashback

Even a Black Hole can have a personality. In a world without rules, there is still tradition. And etiquette. When you pull out of society, you still need a place to hang out. With friends.

You wanna go where everybody knows you're gay.

Far from the surface of The Big Onion, in an obscure corner of downtown, a four-story red brick building leftover from the warehouse era was Home to thousands.

Every weekend its inhabitants would toss off soirée after bash after debauched shindig. To be invited, you merely had to be well dressed, superbly coifed, famous, infamous, filthy rich, devastatingly beautiful, near-naked, encased in plastic, dripping in chains, balanced on spikes that could kill, a fabulous dancer, an exhibitionist, a voyeur, a swinger, a drug dealer, sleeping with the deejay, a go-go speaker boy, a muscle boy, a pretty boy, a boy, a model, a punk rocker, a jock, a dyke, a fag, a faghag, a draghag, straight, bi, celibate, sexy, aloof, brooding, mysterious, scary, extreme, tireless...

Even then, you had to be prepared to wait in a line stretching as far as The Foxy Lady Disco Dancing Lounge for an hour or more. And name-drop your way through the front door.

Unless you were a Queen.

Then you could show up whenever your nail polish finally

dried, unfold yourself from your taxi, and waltz in the front door of the club, past the lineups of commoners, knowing that they were all envious of the ease of entry, the familiarity of fame, the drama. Of Drag.

It was a world where *we* wrote the rulebook.

It was *us* they came to see: the Stars of the Underground.

And we never disappointed.

Monday to Friday was spent planning, sewing, trying on, color draping and stockpiling narcotics. Even if you weren't planning to crank, dressing up was a major event. We had reputations to uphold. As freaks, we *were* the show. It was our responsibility to be bigger than life, and we took that challenge seriously.

The plebeians depended on us.

Our schedule was strict, the itinerary regimented:

FRIDAY:

2:00 p.m. Awake.

4:00 p.m. Awake again. Get up.

4:30 p.m. Remove last night's makeup.

5:30 p.m. Put on makeup to cover makeup that won't come off. Go buy cigarettes.

6:30 p.m. Count the acid. Plan the dose.

7:30 p.m. Awake. The cigarette has burned a hole in the couch.

8:30 p.m. Remove makeup. Shave. Moisturize. Begin applying Night Makeup.

0:30 p.m. Face completed. Search drag room for anything to wear. Find Lulu's black bathing suit for her. Pick out the silver lame palazzo pants for yourself.0

11:00 p.m. Accessorize. It's the only thing that separates us from the lower animals.

11:30 p.m. Light a joint. Call a cab.

Midnight: ARRIVE! Step out of the cab, adjust your skirt, scream

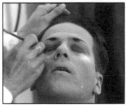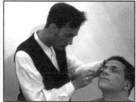

Kim Burly and Gloria. As soon as I got to Edmonton, I immediately grew my hair long enough not to need wigs, and didn't cut it again until the 90s.

with joy, say something funny to the poor straight kids in the lineup, breeze past them, say hi to the Reverend Brother Bob, push through the crowd, dump your furs in the office, sneak up behind a bartender and grab his ass, get him to freepour a scotch, don't write it on your tab, spot the Girls over by the dance floor, strut through the crowd, receive compliments, oh my god I love this song let's dance, who's got the poppers, no, up here, I want everyone to see this outfit, get off the speaker

Gloria and Twiggy in the drag room, 1987
I never could put on my own lashes

bitch we live here, isn't that the Razzberries, where did all these Barry-T wannabees come from, it's like a Barbie convention only hideous, Donna Summer is so fabulous, isn't she, I know we're supposed to hate her now but the music!

12:45 a.m. Meet in the ladies' can at the prearranged time, in the handicapped cubicle. Squeeze everyone in. Sit on the floor, screaming with laughter at absolutely anything. Drop the acid. Pass around the hair spray. Stay until some dyke kicks you all out for reinforcing negative stereotypes of women.

1:00 a.m. Get that feeling in your stomach that lets you know your drugs are working. Get more scotch. Sit high on the bar with your legs crossed so you can torment straight boys. Watch the dance floor like it's a campfire, flickering and flashing and undulating and hypnotizing. Cheer as two guys in muscle shirts climb on a speaker and start tearing off each other's clothes. The club is full, and the beautiful people keep pouring through the door. Some guy can't take his eyes off your tits so take one out and pat his forehead dry.

Gloria, 1988
I'm on the bar at Flashback, mimicking Cleo's
campaign poster. Behind the bar is Cleo as a boy.

1:15 a.m. Hallucinate. Lulu's talking about something, screaming in your ear. Nod and pretend you can understand her. The guy is now licking your legs. You feel too sorry for him to tell him that you can't feel a thing because you're wearing four pairs of Shoppers Drug Mart pantyhose.
1:30 a.m. Ditch the guy. Find The Girls.
1:45 a.m. Grab Lulu and head to the walk-in beer cooler. Take off your shoes and stand on the cold steel until the swelling in your feet goes down. Once shoes fit again, renew dancing.
2:00 a.m. Last call. Ignore it. You know management.
2:30 a.m. Whine to management for more scotch. Hang out with the bartenders while they count their tips. Make so much noise they kick you out. Leave in a huff.
3:00 a.m. Start looking for a party. If unsuccessful, reconvene in the handicapped stall and start your own.

3:30 a.m. Hang out in the kitchen. Laugh as Gretchen passes out.
4:00 a.m. Decide against calling a cab. You and Lulu have decided to walk home. Head down Jasper Avenue, still in heels, as the sun rises, arm in arm. A van starts circling the block. Then it pulls up beside you. The side door slides open and there's five guys watching you. You cross the street, hoping they'll go away. The van turns and pulls alongside you again. You cross again, and this pisses them off. They pour out of the van and run toward you. Lulu rips her stilettos off her feet. "Weapons, girl!" I do likewise. We swing our heels at men we've never met, hoping it's all a sick joke, but they want blood. Lulu gives it to them. Her stiletto connects with a forehead and blood streams out into his eyes. "C'mon, fuckers, you're not gonna let a couple of queens take you out, are ya?" taunts Lulu, as we dodge blows and swing pumps and scream like warriors. When they run off, wounded, realize how lucky you are to be alive. Realize how lucky you are to be Lulu's friend.
4:30 a.m. Go into the Mac's store and call a cab, even though you only live a block away.
5:00 a.m. Go to bed. Have trouble sleeping. Avoid thinking about your life.
SATURDAY: Rinse. Repeat.

For fifteen years, Flashback remained the Guardian of everything that was avant, cutting edge, or alternative. People didn't get hired, they transmogrified until they belonged. Then they started getting paid. Like a huge talent magnet, it attracted outcasts and thrill-seekers.

If you knew you belonged, you stayed. There was room for many on the ride; over the years, hundreds of queens and fags and leather boys and future celebs passed through its hallowed doors.

Twiggy performing at Flashback, '88ish

Lulu and I were both there when Wayne Gretzky showed up *after* last call and demanded champagne. His then girlfriend, Vicki Moss, was wearing a fake fur (long before it was politically correct to do so). Disco star Sylvester watched a bad drag show one night; Sarah Maclaughlin partied in the office with us while we cashed out; Belinda Carlisle danced all night to Go-Gos tunes; The Nylons wore Lulu's Empress campaign buttons home; Craig Russell let us treat him like the Godmother of all drag; The Jazz Butchers drank like kings; the drummer from Heart pissed off Kim Burly and was removed from behind the bar (she had no idea who he was, even though we had just seen the concert the night before); Mrs. Lougheed tried to check her fur coat during a fashion show, and when she couldn't, the coat-check girl was fired, causing more gossip-column fodder; the Speaker of the Legislative Assembly came in once, and all night we made jokes about dancing on the speaker; Scott Thomp-son of Kids in the Hall talked about himself even more than I did; Long John Baldry would lean on the bar and just watch the action; k.d. lang showed up when her name still contained capital letters; Kurt Browning did a pirouette at the main bar (we wouldn't serve him until he did); Mark Messier dragged his brother in, only to prop him up all night (he drank too many Oralyzers); the Ghermezians tried to butt in line, and Lulu told them they weren't well dressed enough and sent them away; Steve Anthony of Much Music was pretty full of himself for a dwarf; the lead singer of Twisted Sister sent someone to the club to find him a date, so we hooked him up with Tiffany, our most stunning crossdresser; Divine called every time she was in town, looking for marijuana; and any time there was a touring musical or dance show or rodeo finals or large-scale figure skating event in town, the dance floor would be packed with new temporary faces, amazed that you could find a location that decadent on the prairies, amazed that a New York-style disco could exist in the Provinces.

Life in the Fab lane. All you had to do was live through it.

Home. This was where Family could take root, be fruitful, and multiply.

Home.

If ducks ruled the Underground...Gloria rules behind the bar at Flashquack.
The scene in 1988, rendered by Iris in pen, ink and feathers.

"HAVING A WONDERFUL TIME, Mom's a little cranky!"

Iris turns her talents to dinner at home with Mom.
"Mom's a little cranky" as chain-saw Gloria presides over
Ora, Lulu, Tallulah, Iris, Kim Burly and Tina.

Lulu

Creation
Hallowe'en 1982

"Closets are for clothes...lots and lots of fabulous clothes!"
–Lulu LaRude

Flashback. Seconds after witnessing my first drag show, I began the search for my dragmother. I was one of the Lucky Ones. I was adopted immediately. Without a mother figure to take you under her hemline you would merely float on the fringe, looking for a way into the scene. Outsiders themselves, queens are by nature suspicious of outsiders.

Your dragmother became your mentor, model, motivator and finally your main competition if things progressed naturally. Once she had taught you all the tricks in her arsenal, it was in your job description to dethrone her. In the natural scheme of things, there can only be <u>one</u> queen. Like a beehive of court intrigue, the battle to the death was both public and passionate.

One night I saw my drag twin. Immediately, I asked the bartender what her name was.

Lulu LaRude.

When I first met her, it became immediately obvious that we were of the same mold. Both of us were tall, impossibly loud, wild, and had size fourteen shoes. We were like gigantic screaming Barbie dolls with no "off" button. Instantly the scale shifted. With another giant beside you, you don't feel so freakishly tall. Often we were mistaken for each other, in and out of drag. She hadn't been around long, in fact she was fresh off the street (literally), but she took me in like a pro, and together we began terrorizing any show we could bully our way into.

She partied with a queen aptly named ＄rash. The two of them were wild women, creating looks and characters from the refuse of garage sales, back alleys and hardware stores. The night I first laid eyes on them, they were making a one-time-only appearance as Chandelerious and Vivvy Pink: neo-Punk Valley girls decorated with extension chords. Trash (as Vivvy) was wearing a plastic neon striped tablecloth stolen from Earl's, and carried a clear plastic purse filled with live grasshoppers. Lulu's Chandelerious was a camp, drugged out Connie Francis-type creation with a blond hairpiece perched on her head, teased a good seven inches high. Her 50s party dress was shredded, burnt and stained, and held together with staples and safety pins. They floated through Flashback on a Quaalude cloud, connected by cables and chords, outcasts from the Glamour circuit, living a fashion anarchy.

They were like me.

Only free.

I looked at Lulu and knew I had found her. Lulu LaRude became my dragmother.

Trash as Vivvy Pink, 1982

DARRIN HAGEN

We fucked, because that's how you met people back then.

In a sacred ceremony, we did a midnight dip in the giant fountain, visited Purple City, lit a joint off the eternal flame in front of the legislature, and Trash and Lulu anointed me with the name that would immortalize me underground for eternity. I held my breath, probably because I had just had a toke, and waited for The Name.

Gloria Hole.

Not quite what I had pictured.

For the next four years, we spent every minute of every day together. Like family.

Lulu loved life on the edge. It was where she did her best work.

I would watch her putting on her makeup, trying to make sense of the many phases of faces. We drank Southern Comfort (very Janis Joplin) and listened to Midler and would head to the bar, or I would drop her off on the Strip by the Holiday Inn and wait for her at the bar, where she would tell tales of perverts and freaks, laughing about the fights she sometimes had to get into. One of her favorite lines once she had the trick's money was "By the way, I'm a queen. I hope you don't mind."

Most of them didn't. Men usually don't.

Her sense of humor had a mean streak. When I was fighting with my psychotic faghag roommate one day, Lulu suddenly jumped into the argument.

"Gloria, it's her birthday. Don't be mean to Shirley." I was about to shoot back something mean when I saw a glint in her eye. So I sat and watched as Lulu won Shirley over.

"Let me do your makeup for your birthday dinner. It'll be my present to you." I watched as Lulu painted the heaviest whore face I've ever witnessed, keeping a straight face as she cooed over Shirley's "classic bone structure". Shirley left for her date, the door closed behind her, and Lulu burst out laughing.

"She didn't even look in the mirror!" she howled.

I realized how lucky I was that she was my friend.

Eventually we got thrown out of that apartment. Lulu moved in with Ricky and I started camping on Deejay's couch. Deejay was a Satanist. I slept in her altar, surrounded by black candles, black velvet paintings of the devil, and books on black magic. Lulu was never far away, though, and when the witch stuff started to freak me out, Lulu and I moved into a house together with Annie Hole and Joolz, two diametrically opposed women who worked at Flashback. The one thing we all had in common was a bad attitude towards the world. We were antisocialites. Joining us on occasion were members of a Cowtown gang: Flora Tron, Guy, Ty Morgan, and a larger-than-life queen trapped in a woman's body named $\mathbb{S}$ister $\mathbb{N}$eon.

As long as the drugs flowed, we were happy; strolling through our neighborhood connected by chains, draped in leopard print, mohawks pointing angrily to the sky. Annie supervised the proceedings, the reincarnation of Nina Hagen, her black lips sucking on a Virginia Slim while she cued up the vinyl. We liked our music loud and annoying.

We frightened people.

We weren't drag queens; we were Dragon Queens. Separately, Lulu and I were manageable; together, never.

We made a pact: we would be next. Together, we could rule this town. The Big Onion was ours for the taking.

Well, almost.

This game was ruled by tradition. Like any age-old ritual, it had rules and etiquette. Crowns garnered respect.

Lulu and Neon, on the 10 year anniversary of Lulu's reign as Empress.

We had to be crowned to make it official.

Not an easy task; Lulu needed to get off the street and get a real job (hooker didn't look good on the application form for Empress) and I hadn't even done my first drag show yet. But everyone around me knew it was only a matter of time.

They knew a queen when they saw one.

So night after night, I danced on

the speakers, performing every song that got played. When my first big break came, it wasn't from Lulu. She was still pretty much an outsider. I was asked by the reigning Empress, Mrs. K., to perform in the next show. Only one stip-ulation: I had to do it in black drag.

Before the polit-ically correct amongst you fly off the handle, let me explain: most of the world's best drag music is sung by black women. We relived the lives of these tormented divas through their amazing music: pumps planted on the stage, gospel-inspired vocals tearing

Lulu and Gloria, 1983. The Dragon Queens' first photo shoot. The apple doesn't fall very far from the tree.

through our souls...it remains, to this day, the best lip-synching material around. So for us to do a whole show in black drag was the biggest gift we could give back to these ladies who had given us so much. Not to mention it was a lot of work, and black panstick was expensive. Also, realize that I'm not talking about Al Jolson with white lips and gloves to match. If there was one thing these queens knew, it was their makeup technique.

I sat in a chair in the drag room, looking at the creation in the mirror.

Lindee had done an amazing job. A tall, beautiful, Amazon goddess looked back with my own eyes. (Author's note: photographic evidence does not verify this claim.) I watched her closely, discovering her facial expressions, examining her from every angle, like recognizing a total stranger. I was terrified to go on stage. She, however, had been ready all her life.

I remember my knees shaking as I stood in my new slingbacks. I remember the music: "It's Raining Men" by The Weather Girls. I remember thinking that nothing would be the same after this moment.

I remember how lucky I felt. I remember...

...the Applause.

At the party afterward I saw the way the past monarchs were treated. With respect.

Crowns garnered respect.

Around this time, a strip agent that we partied with offered us our first professional gig. She wanted to start booking drag acts in lieu of the strippers that she usually sent to bars. Even though my drag career was less than a week old, Lulu and I said yes and started to put together a show.

"If you're gonna do this, we might as well go buy you some real tits," she said. I had "borrowed" hers for my debut, but we were both in this show, so we needed two sets. We went to the bra department at Woodwards and searched for a saleslady. After standing around being ignored for fifteen minutes, we approached an older, non-threatening, matronly woman.

"Can you show us where your prosthetic breasts are?" asked Lulu as if it were the most natural thing in the world. The saleslady didn't bat an eye.

"Certainly," she said efficiently, and led us to the back of the department. She went to a set of small drawers set dis-creetly into the wall, opened one, took out a decorator box, opened it and removed a velvet bag with a drawstring, opened it and took out something wrapped in bubble plastic. She unwrapped the plastic, and proudly displayed the breast.

"It's only $450. Top of the line."

Lulu and I looked at each other, trying not to laugh. The saleslady was only trying to be helpful, but she had clearly misunderstood.

Lulu smiled and, without missing a beat, said, "Have you got anything in foam?"

We were very practical girls, in many ways.

A week later, we stood on a tavern stage in front of a grimly silent bunch of straight farmers in Gibbons, Alberta, population 2335. They had all showed up looking for naked female flesh, and were instead presented with two six-foot eight amateur drag queens lip-synching to a loud ghetto-blaster. When some of the drunker patrons began screaming they wanted to see some tits, Lulu pulled out her foamies and threw them onto his table.

"Here, you can hold onto these. Now shut your hole, honey,

DARRIN HAGEN

'cause mine's making money." The audience howled. The heckler even laughed. It was my first experience with the power of shock, of turning the tables and making your freak status into a weapon. It seemed life on the street had prepared Lulu for anything. Especially dealing with hostile men. Gradually the mood shifted from hostility to mild amusement, and by the end of the show, they were even clapping. We each made fifty bucks. It was the first time I got paid for doing drag. On the way home, Lulu said, "We have to tell everybody how fabulous it was, or they'll never let us hear the end of it." We got to the club and boasted of our triumph, and suddenly we were professional queens.

Perception is nine-tenths of reality.

Now that Lulu had a source of income (I had also gotten her a job at Flashback), and we were approaching legitimate queenliness, we decided we needed a crown. Each. This wasn't just us being greedy–there were several crowns up for grabs. Just pick one and go for it.

Lulu decided to run for Empress. Her campaign image was "Tootsie". Lulu would arrive in a smart, businessy power skirt, complete with sensible red hair and glasses. I was her campaign manager. We were nineteen.

She lost to an Old Guard Dowager, Mary Mess.

Tradition stated that the Runner-Up would always be appointed the title ofsecond-in-line to the throne: Lulu became the eighth Imperial Princess.

But not before the first Empress chewed her out for wearing jeans to a campaign show, the second Empress and I got in a fist fight, while Empresses three through seven just generally scowled their disapproval. They were not amused.

Lulu and I didn't do traditional drag. We took our cue from Trash, who had risen from the genderfuck depths to become Mz. Flashback on little more than pure imagination. Crowds adored her even though she had never donned an evening gown.

She was our inspiration.

Trash

DARRIN HAGEN

One Man's Garbage...

1983

"I love a parade!"
−Trash

What we throw out defines us; what we leave behind, even more so.

Trash had been a nomad from an early age, as long as anyone could remember. She floated into town an unknown and was soon a regular fixture on the Hill, where tough boys and pretty boys and Indian boys merged to party, scrap, buy, and sell. Sixteen going on a thousand in experience; young but frighteningly wise.

She spent her life casting off the things life collects as you live it. Refusing to be tied down by conventions of home, she moved often, shedding furniture and drag, leaving stuff in alleys and apartments.

Trash was one of our primary influences. Bravado to the *nth* degree, dressing out of Hardware as much as Women's Wear. Drag was an intensely public experience for Trash, whose motto was "It's not worth doing if you can't freak out some straight boys." So on Hallowe'en, rather than doing a show in the bar, she would crank it up loud and head to Victor's (a swanky downtown eatery), and drink free scotch from drunk businessmen horny enough to be confused by her trollopy... well, Trashy presence. She was public enough that gossip columnists often commented on her presence at events like Klondike Days, where she scandalized the midway, or reported her legendary battles with her Mr. Flashback. We all read it in the news when Trash resigned her title because she wasn't cast as Marilyn in the Dead Celebrities Hallowe'en show.

...Bianca Bang-Bang, who *was* playing Marilyn—this was the first drag show I ever saw. Note the dress...

She hung the crown in a 7-11 bag on the apartment doorknob of Bianca Bang-Bang, who *was* playing Marilyn, and headed out for the night in drag.

And did her own show.

Somewhere.

Living randomly, as Trash did, turned the city streets into a canvas. Not content to perform on-stage, she took her unique brand of Anti-fashion out for strolls. While there, she could furnish her life from the discarded treasures of civilians. Her dwelling was always an experience unto itself: found couches, scavenged lamps, coffee tables made of shards of broken mirror balanced on cement chunks and railway ties. As Trash was only five-seven, it was often a mystery as to how she actually transported some of these monoliths back to home base, but she wasn't the type to let something as trivial as physics keep her from decorating her world.

She was the first Live Art I had ever met.

One day Lulu and I sat on a low brick wall, watching the endlessly boring K-Days parade schlep past. It was about to rain, as it always did, and we were bored, as we usually were. A discordant marching band shuffled past, clutching their sheet music as a huge gust of wind threatened to scatter the melodies across the sky. Lulu and I passed a joint back and forth, giggling about how funny straight people were when they tried to stage a big event. The most glamorous thing we had seen so far was the Klondike Kate convertible, and frankly, we had better fashion sense.

Suddenly a scream was heard from three blocks away. Not a scream of fear or warning as much as a scream of announcement, of arrival. Everyone around us looked in the direction of the scream. There, walking towards us, in a drugged out crinoline cloud, feathers in her hair, dress cut down to there, a banner across her foamies that read "Klondike Queen", tossing Flashback swizzlesticks at the children, was Trash.

Lulu and I screamed with laughter, then shouted to her. She heard, looked over to us with a glint in her eye, and joined us on the wall. Together, we laughed at the parade, laughed at people staring at us, laughed as Trash filled us in on her exploits of the afternoon.

"I did a hit of acid and decided it was a good day for a parade. I didn't even know there was already one happening! So I just joined in." She started bragging about the boys she had been tormenting as she trolloped through her afternoon. It was always kind of hard to believe that any guy would be fooled by someone dressed like she was, but as I sat there, disbelieving, Lulu shushed both of us and said, "Jocks in convertibles: three o'clock."

"Chomp," we all agreed under our breath.

A moment of reverent silence as the beefcake float drove closer. They were Oilers or Eskimos or something butch like that, I've never been able to tell them apart. Just as they pulled past us, Trash screamed "Hi, honey! Give a girl a lift?"

The Jocks all looked in her direction and waved, then one of them motioned for her to get in.

"That's my cue, see ya later!" She jumped off the low wall, navigated through a bunch of kids, then trotted as fast as she could manage in those heels after the motorcade, as Lulu and I sat silent, our jaws hanging wide open.

The jock's face changed expression gradually as Trash drew closer. Remember, distance is a girl's best friend. She probably looked fairly alluring from across the street, but up-close drag reality in daylight is a sobering thing.

No one can blend *that* well.

By the time the jock figured out what he was dealing with, it was too late. Trash had climbed into the convertible and sat high on the back, waving like the perfect pageant winner. Short of physically tossing her onto the asphalt, there wasn't a lot he could do. The last thing he needed was a photo of him roughing up what looked a woman, albeit a garishly dressed one.

As they drove away, we saw Trash put her gloved hand on the jock's knee. He did nothing; just sat, staring straight ahead as his buddies howled with laughter.

Lulu and I sat in awe. "Go, girl," we whispered admiringly. Silently, we saluted, giving the Royal Wave: hat-2-3, purse-2-3, pearls-2-3, wave and rest.

Gloria and Lulu: a classic daughter and mother portrait

DARRIN HAGEN

Forego The Fabulous
And Embrace Anarchy
1984-1985

"I always wanted my name in the papers."
—Gloria Hole

ulu and I shopped at Value Village, had weird hair and would wear anything:
Garbage bags and rhinestones.
Plastic wrap with high heels.
I specialized in lampshade hats with hairpieces flowing out of them, and vintage cat-eye glasses. Waitress uniforms. Lulu was a little sleazier, catsuits and mohawks, sink plugs for earrings.

There was a touch of road warrior in everything we did.

We decided that our route to fame was a simple one: just be the weirdest people in the world and the world would be our oyster. We'd stroll down Jasper Avenue, singing "Cry Me A River" in full-throttle falsetto, ignoring the stares from passers-by. It was our favorite song. We'd get on a bus with our dollar bill fare rolled up and sticking out of our noses. It was powerful being that bizarre; people would immediately turn away, or get furious. To see an old man start cursing us just for singing and choreographing while waiting for a bus was an interesting view of lines of tolerance. Some folks get mad just because you're not like them.

One morning, in protest of the new, earlier toilet-cleaning schedule, we went to work in our pajamas. It got a big laugh as we swept floors in floppy slippers, but of course one thing led to another, and we ended up partying in our pajamas for two days at an M.D.A. party. We passed out.

In the morning there was a phone call from the club. My parents had been trying to get a hold of me for hours, my boss informed me. My piano had arrived.

I struggled for a moment with this information. "Oh my God, is it Thanksgiving?" I moaned. I had told Mom and Dad that now that I was living in a house, I wanted my piano. They had driven it to Edmonton and had been waiting in the front yard of the house for two hours.

We called a cab, grabbed a couple of burly fags from the party and flew home like the wind.

Mom's first view of Lulu was her slippered foot as she stepped out of the cab. Then I emerged. We had been in our pajamas for two and a half days, and both wore sunglasses to hide our vibrating pupils.

We hauled my upright up the steps, my Dad and four fags.

Inside the house, it became a distracting game of keeping Dad's attention from wandering to the elaborately framed drag photos of us on the mantel. I played for the first time in two years. Fingers slid magically into place, just like when I lived in Rocky. The room filled with the sounds of my favorite, dear, treasured friend.

I hadn't realized how much I had missed it.

Lulu and I were now regulars on the Flashback stage. The management didn't really get along with the reigning Mz., so we just started turning ourselves into stars. We would hang out on the loading dock, tormenting people

Gloria and Lulu take the stage.
Facing page: Gloria in several fetching outfits.

DARRIN HAGEN

and waving and hooting at the police when they cruised by. Lulu would hold the joint high and scream "Yoo-hoo! Husbands!" like she was daring them to arrest her. When I asked why she wasn't more careful she answered, "If they want to search you, tell them you're a sex change and they have to send for a female cop. Most won't bother." We treated Flashback like our own private playground.

It was simple: no one ever said no.

Our first big show with our names on the poster was called "The Wild Sorority Sisters From The Planet Playtex Proudly Present: A Salute to Trailercourt Women." Our first real duet we did together was "Cry Me A River", closed captioned for the thinking impaired (which meant I acted out every word in a made-up sign language). The act was designed to be a parody of Lindee Star and her twin brother, who would perform in real sign language. The effect was lovely (the first two or three thousand times), but Lulu and I usually had the most fun when it was at other people's expense. So we put our own version on stage, anticipating rage from the Old Guard for making fun of them.

That performance launched us into infamy.

The Empress Club didn't get it. But the audiences did.

The sight of Lulu lip-synching into a lime green toilet brush or me teaching her how to give head on a

Gloria

Lulu

We were very practical girls in many ways...

zucchini won us quick acclaim.

But we weren't really crown material.

Yet.

So for a whole year we pushed limits, challenged Drag Authority, crossed every line of taste, and took over. The ruling Mz. Flashback was so scared of us that she ran from her own stage. We ran right on behind her and established a kind of renegade royalty: unelected but so firmly supported by the audience that no one dared challenge our authority.

We immediately set the plans in motion for our official arrival: May long weekend. The Coronation of the ninth Mz. Flashback.

I would be that Mz. Flashback.

Or at least, that was the plan.

It wasn't as easy as we thought. A talented nobody named Twiggy almost beat me. But on voting night, I unleashed my secret weapon.

My number on voting night was a Sonny & Cher song. "I Got You, Babe". It was performed just like the end of their t.v. show: Mr. K. played Sonny and I was Cher, albeit a bargain basement version. Our costumes hadn't shown up and we were in a panic, throwing on whatever we could find in the knee-deep pile of tattered gowns that was the costume pit. We hit the stage

DARRIN HAGEN

desperate: Twiggy had received a huge round of applause for her performance. I had to top that or all of our carefully laid plans would be for nothing.

The music started. The crowd cheered as soon as they recognized the music, then screamed with laughter when the spotlight hit us. We looked like a bad Vegas version of a watered down caricature of a parody of Sonny & Cher. But that was fine: we knew our words and we launched into the routine with conviction, pretending we had meant to look that way, knowing all the while that we had the Mother of all big finishes in store.

We were nearing the end. The crowd was still with us. Then the loudest scream I've heard in my life erupted as our secret weapon hit the stage: Chastity.

Actually, a midget in drag dressed as Chastity.

Gloria: The Value Village fashion show

The roar from the crowd obliterated the music completely. We stood on that stage, picked Chastity up in our arms, and smiled, like the perfect t.v. family. Chastity's monster sucker got stuck in my black wig and hung there, like a sticky, sugary earring.

We had crossed every line of taste in the book. And we won. That night I was crowned Mz. Flashback IX.

Standing on that stage, hair sculpted, lips quivering, arms stretched out at the standup mike, the spotlight cascading down then breaking like a million mirrors, refracted by my jewels until they were blinded, my eyes gazing upwards, sparkling with life and emotion and passion for my separateness, my existence, that moment, as if my entire life culminated on that stage, in that moment...

...that shining, perfect moment...

...the Applause.

With the crown on my head, we all piled into a big green van that had moved every drag queen in town at some point, and headed out to our first Tofield party.

You may want to pause and picture a convoy of wildly adorned she-males racing East to a rural setting to do the wildest drag show around. Legends abounded, tied together by traditions that went back to the house of Millicent herself. And the new Mz. Flashback was the Annual Guest of Honour.

The farm belonged to Rhoda B. and two lesbians. A modest place, but that part of the country saw some things that most farms can't even imagine. The house was a series of granaries and small trailers, attached in a crooked line with doors knocked out between them.

That night, as Lulu and I stood beside a bonfire so hot our bangs melted, guzzling Grand Marnier out of the bottle, our high heels sinking into the earth, she warned, "Whatever you do, don't pass out tonight. Evil events await the Mz. who cannot remain conscious throughout her Coronation." This wasn't going to be easy, as a good drag campaign is equal parts exhaustion, inspiration, and hallucination. It had been an entire week of shaving, cranking, painting and not sleeping. Already I was having trouble maintaining a vertical position without a birch to cling to.

Dozens of fags, dykes, and freaks wandered through the dark, back and forth between vans and campers, smoking drugs in the treehouse, and apparently there was an orgy in the barn. But we had a show to do.

Gloria
...that shining, perfect moment...the Applause.

We made our way to the stage. When I saw it, my jaw dropped.

In a hollow in a field was a swampy dugout, four or five feet deep. The surface was thick with a dark green algae, the odd bulrush poking up out of the murky water. Around the pond a dozen cars and trucks parked facing the water with their headlights blazing a makeshift spotlight. In the center of the dugout was the stage: a floating raft of oil drums and plywood connected to the mainland by a long 2x4. On the raft stood Amii L. Nitrate, balancing precariously as she gesticulated, a full two seconds behind the tinny strains of "Somewhere Over The Rainbow" emanating full-blast from a car stereo. The last thing I remember was Ginger Snot taking the big plunge in a wedding dress.

Bianca Bang-Bang said it best: "I know I'm in the country, but what country?"

I awoke with a start, hours later. Still in drag, in someone's living room, on someone's couch. A quick feel to the top of my head confirmed the worst.

My crown was gone.

I hastily searched the remnants of memories from the night before and came up empty. Then I heard laughter and realized there were people watching me. I looked around and saw Trash and Lulu, evil smirks on their faces.

"Lose something, Gloria?"

They led me back across the gravel road to the farm. A cow wearing a Dolly Parton wig ruminated glumly, watching us as we made our way to the chicken coop. There, glinting and sparkling in the early morning sunlight, high atop a power pole, sat the official Mz. Flashback crown. Thirty feet up.

I climbed up, like eight Mz. Flashbacks before me, and retrieved my prize.

I was one of them.

Sometime that same day, I read the beginning of the Creation of the Hole Family on a wall in the outhouse, penned by Ginger Snot sometime before she hit the brink in the dugout. Her stained wedding dress flapped on the clothesline.

The journey was underway.

If we could now get Lulu elected, we could control every drag event on every Big Onion stage for three solid years.

We could build a drag dynasty of entertainers that could

Skeleton Funnies at Flashback:
Gloria, Twiggy and Dorky   Twiggy
Water damage gives these photos a certain *je ne sais quoi*...
and how do you tell the queens from the audience on Hallowe'en?

rule the Big Onion for years to come. So we adopted queens left
and right and created: The Hole Family.

And every once in a while — you created a monster.

And of course, it happened one Hallowe'en.

Excretia

DARRIN HAGEN

It Happened One Hallowe'en

1984

"Never turn your back on her, you stupid girl!"
—Trash

Lulu and I should have known you couldn't toy with the dark forces, especially on a night as potent as this. Were we playing Goddess? Perhaps. But like the most well meaning of scientists, we were trying to use our powers for good and not for evil.

Girls just wanna have fun.

So we talked a mild mannered Maritime boy into crossing the line.

He didn't have to worry about a thing. We would personally supervise the transformation. With our combined talents and access to the Flashback costume pit, we would shape him into the most potent of punk priestesses. Lulu and I liked to believe we were the cutting edge of genderfuck drag. We would create her in our own image and send her forth to fly with the freaks.

O, the arrogance. Outmothering mother nature is pure folly.

When we stepped back to survey our creation, a cold chill swept the room.

For there stood evil incarnate.

Fishnets shredded, then tied back together in a haphazard web. Tight black spandex mini. Bare midriff with a lean washboard stomach. Black lipstick. Black mask eye makeup and black cheekbones. White skin. A tire tube necklace with spikes protruding. Women's athletic hockey padding spray painted black with studs and rivets and bolts instead of beads. Ripped fingerless evening gloves and black dragonlady nails.

Before us stood the Spawn of Satan in stilettos. Like Frankenstein's fantasy bride, her hair swept straight up in a manic mohawk, reaching for heaven but rooted in Hell.

Then, like a low menacing growl from the very depths of depravity rising to the surface of our collective consciousness, her name sprung from our lips. Before we knew it, it had been spoken aloud, like a Spite released from Pandora's box. Irretrievable. Irrevocable. Unstoppable.

Excretia.

Excretia Nefarious Vulgaris. Keeper of the Royal Obscenities and Something Unspeakably Wicked. The Nuclear Waste Poster Child for the Nineties.

Under that calm male exterior seethed and bubbled a rage that, once unleashed, ran rampant through the night. Lulu and I gulped, and then did what all mad scientists must do.

We abandoned our creation and ran. Condemn us if you must. It was beyond our control.

That night she perched high on one of the standup bars like a garish gargoyle, shrieking huge swelling opera diva screams over the pulsating technobeat, pausing to cross her eyes, then flick a burning cigarette over the heads of the crowd. A beer bottle, when emptied, would be lobbed over her shoulder and into the mob. The world became her garbage can, a place to purge the piss and rage and fury and disgust with Life. The Universe. Everything.

Excretia didn't hate straight people. She thought everyone should own a couple. She lived to frighten them, and would do whatever it took.

Within a year, her name struck terror in the hearts of every hetero that walked into the place.

The World was Fucked. And she was proof.

That night she reduced three straight chicks to tears, almost got punched out by one of their boyfriends, and stood in the bar lineup burning holes in some woman's fur coat while she chatted up her date.

Dragzilla on drugs. And we were Tokyo.

That night, she was born. Again.

That night she also picked up a cute straight boy while his girlfriend wasn't looking and sucked him off in the downstairs can. They found him sitting unconscious on a toilet, jeans pulled down to his ankles, a ring of black lipstick around the base of his dick.

Life can be so ironic.

Strangely enough, some people were drawn to her seductively vile ways. The sheer sense of abandon in her tornado of terror sucked in the masochists one after another. She became the Demon Dominatrix, hypnotizing the unsuspecting like a Mad Max Medusa. Caught unawares, they found themselves in the arms of something wild and scary. Alien sex fiend on the hunt. Submit.

When Excretia disrupted our shows we stopped asking her to do them. But she didn't need the stage to perform. The Underground was her stage.

Excretia also fought with her own Drag Demon. With alarming regularity, she would swear off the whole scene, sometimes going as far as to burn all her drag, like she was exorcising the spirits that made her dress up.

But if it were that easy to quit, many of us would already have done just that.

The following Saturday would see her lurking near the dance floor, in a new outfit, chains rattling as she swayed, then thrashed to the music. We would all look the other way, hoping no one would point an accusing finger at us for not realizing the Fury we had set in motion.

Excretia, 1983

Finally she wearied of us and moved to Toronto to terrorize a whole new chunk of the world.

She scared us queens as much as anybody else.

Creation comes with a certain responsibility.

Photos of Millie in drag are rare: here she is, centre,
flanked by Dorky and Twiggy on the right, Buster Box and Tallulah on the left,
at Flora's ball in Calgary, 1986

In The Beginning

"I'm Number One!"
—Empress I Millie

People always prefer talking about you when you're gone.

Upon my arrival in River City, my impressionable young mind was instantly deluged with a Noah-style flood of legends, myths, and glorious memories of faded grandeur.

It all began many moons ago when an Indian Princess planted her heel in the earth and declared herself Queen. Inspired by her might, hordes fell in behind her to cultivate the seeds of independence.

That Queen had a name.

Millicent.

She would be the only queen to simultaneously wear the Two Crowns of the Underground. And she would remind you of it every time she remembered it.

When Flashback was born, Millie was there, putting her name on the membership list before the paint on the dance floor had dried. By year's end she had established two thrones and was firmly seated on both. For her efforts, she was immortalized.

Empress I, Mz. Flashback I, the pushiest queen around: all still kowtowed to Millie. She was Unofficial Godmother to every queen I had ever met, partied with or slept with. She was the Spirit of the Supremes half-bred with a shot of Indian Princess, shaken over ice, two straws. She breezed through every front door with the ease of a mountain wind, as familiar as sunlight. Drinks appeared like spirits on the bar in front of her, where her thin arms rested, manicured hand guiding a butch cigarette to her mouth, exhaling smoke signals to the patrons around her.

She held court wherever she sat, creating a powwow of activity. Millie, being Number One, cherished all that she spawned. She called you by number, not by name, like a worried hen constantly taking attendance. She took an indirect kind of credit for every crowned queen in the Big Onion.

The party years had taken their toll on Millie, who was nearly forty when I met her. I had guessed her age much higher; I hadn't learned yet that age was relative. She strolled through downtown as if she owned it, but of course no one that saw her knew that. They saw only a tired-looking Indian man, like a hundred others you would see in a day. The only clue to her royal past was her nails, her pride and joy. They were long and immaculately manicured, at odds with her otherwise pedestrian appearance.

For Millie, the highest honor in the land was to be Empress. Or Mz. Flashback. The second you achieved either, your worth multiplied in her eyes. But as far as she was concerned, no one had ever been quite as fabulous as she remembered herself being. And because most of us were in grade school the first time she donned a frock, we were in no position to argue.

I would nod and smile whenever Millie boasted of her grandeur, not disbelieving, but skeptical. It was difficult to match the Myth with the frail man I saw in front of me. Then at a party at her home, when she still had one, Millie pulled me to one side, secretively. She opened a photo album and showed me a black and white portrait of herself.

She was beautiful.

She wasn't in drag in the photograph. But she was a Queen.

Some men don't need to wear makeup to unleash their feminine side. I saw a proud, arrogant sideways glance at the camera, a tilt of the head, high sharp cheekbones, the hands placed just so. The attitude dripped off the image.

The Indians have a term for that: "two-spirited".

I recognized the look: I had seen it many times in my own mirror as I tried to discover what I was. I realized the only thing separating us was a few thousand bottles of rye.

Millie never really recovered from being Queen. Her year had been particularly rough: weeks after she and her Emperor had been crowned, he was arrested and charged with murder for some S/M sex that got out of hand. Millie, undaunted, finished her reign alone. Kingless. Regina Glorianna. Like Elizabeth I, Millie believed men were useful for guarding the crown, not possessing it.

She sat alone at her ball, throne cen-tre stage. It was how everybody remembered her. Number One.

The candidates for the throne that year were Chatty Cathy Jackson and Grindl. Chatty was swept to power, and Grindl, who had also lost the first Empress competition, died later that year under a table at a drunken party. Everyone thought that she had merely passed out, and continued to party around her. Hours later, when someone bothered to check, they finally called an ambulance and toasted her one last time.

Millie on the right, in a characteristic pose. On the left, the blond boy who won Gloria's heart...

Chatty went on to become the first Entertainer of the Year, and then the first Entertainer of the Decade. Millie went on to become the eternal dowager.

In her wake came all sixteen of us. The Empresses: Chatty Cathy Jackson, Nikki, Rayette, Trixie, Lindee Star, Mrs. K., Mary Mess, and Lulu LaRude. The Mz. Flashbacks: Felicia, Gino, Bianca Bang-Bang, Tina, Trash, Lexy Con and Gloria Hole.

By the time I became Number Nine, as she called me, Millie had stumbled down a few steps on the social ladder. Alcohol was rapidly becoming her main pastime. She no longer owned her own business; in fact she had taken a position as co-toilet scrubber with Lulu and I at the club. Us "new girls" at the bar were amused, to say the least, and Millie put up with more than her share of queen bitchiness. Dorky and I would draw little teepees and tomahawks on her time card. We constantly teased her about her age, and we never missed a chance to make fun of Diana Ross, Millie's idol.

Millie never fought back, just threatened revenge now and then.

We laughed, thinking that she would never bother.

Gloria

A Legend
In Her Own Lunchtime

"No one deserves this more than you do...
except maybe me."

–Lulu Larude

A good queen was judged almost entirely on the last week of her year of rule: Step-down Week. As the reigning Mz. Flashback prepared to bid her public farewell, the new candidates battled in the wings, ready to assume power.

Campaign Week.

This ritual was an intense one for several reasons. It was a double-edged kind of mood; relief and nostalgia; glory and sadness; the bittersweet feeling of something that feels so good, yet can't be over already, yet has to be.

Going out in style was the whole point.

Two Divas with tiaras on their minds, battling publicly to rule the Underground: the ingredients of an exciting war. The public swarmed in behind their favorite, and the Battle Royale was underway.

The intensity of the experience was multiplied by the schedule: a manic, mesmerizing mayhem of nerves, passion and drugs. The sheer number of shows in a campaign week was enough to make a hardened diva tremble.

The excitement all took place during the week leading up to the May long weekend, but preparations began back in March. First, to ensure the integrity of the Crown, some candidates had to be drummed up.

This choice had to be made carefully. Talent, youth and personality all had to be balanced with a real desire to represent the Club in the fashion to which it had become accustomed.

Flashback had the best queens, bar none. From the Grandeur of Millie to the Wildness of Felicia, from the Seduction of Gino to the High-Voltage Energy of Bianca Bang-Bang, from the Artistry of Gracie to the Cult of Personality that was Tina, through the Insanity that was Trash, and finally to the Timid Glamour of Lexy, the lure of the title of Mz. Flashback proved stronger than a young man's common sense or willpower year after year.

It wasn't just about the Crown, either.

The ranks of Flashback queens had a rich, varied history, and a nationwide reputation for performance on the edge. Many of the past rulers still performed, and when they hit the stage, confident that they no longer had anything to prove, the crowd cheered maniacally.

Those queens represented not just a fag bar, but a whole way of life: intense, popular, beautiful, mad, proud, and more fashionable than God ever intended.

When I stepped into the well-worn, hallowed pumps of my foresisters, Flashback was nearing the end of its first decade. A year later, the world was a different place. I was a different queen.

Power changes everything.

Lulu and I decided that nobody else was ready for that kind of power...

DARRIN HAGEN

Lulu and I decided that nobody else was ready for that kind of power. As long as we controlled the Flashback stage, the Big Onion queens would be answerable to us. Lulu was becoming a phenomenon. She learned quickly what audiences were looking for and delivered it with feeling. She was the perfect blend of imagination, talent, with a touch of tragic heroine thrown in for dramatic effect. Her rise from the gutter touched people, and she had become the anchor of any show she performed in. I, on the other hand, was rapidly becoming the comic queen. Lulu and I hatched up some of the most demented performance drag anyone had seen. Our sphere of influence spread to Calgary, where we met the New Guard of the South. A wild family had also taken root there: The Del Rockos. Soon the Holes and the Del Rockos were inseparable. Flora Tron, Justine Tyme, Guy and Neon were changing the face of drag in the south. Cowtown, already cutting edge, went crazy when the Big Onion girls performed. Regular field trips between the cities strengthened our position as the premier entertainment dynasty in Alberta. Finally, Lindee Star relented and awarded Lulu Entertainer of the Year. (Actually, she sold it to Lulu for a dollar at the Calgary Ball as they stood stealing jewelry from some Vancouver queen.)

We sat in the drag pit one day, laying our plans.

"All we have to do," Lulu said, "is make sure the next Mz. Flashback is a member of the Family. She would still have to win the pageant on her own, but we could groom and assist her. Carefully," she added, remembering Excretia.

She took a huge drag off the joint we were smoking, then doubled over, coughing. This was normal. Then she refused the next toke. This was not. Complaining of a pain in her chest, she went back to cleaning toilets. (This was how we subsidized our drag habit: commercial sanitary engineers. Hardly glamorous, but essentially we got paid for cleaning up our own mess.)

Half an hour later, the pain still hadn't subsided.

When we got her to the hospital, we were told that one of her lungs had collapsed. She was admitted instantly.

The timing couldn't have been worse. Lulu's campaign for Empress IX was merely a month away, and she had a major public appearance coming up, playing Marilyn in a hair show. I immediately phoned Lindee Star to tell her the bad news: Lulu would have to be replaced.

Some Edmonton Queens (1)

Sister Neon's family changed the face of drag in Cowtown,
then she took The Big Onion by storm.

Kim Burly: who says you can't be glamorous in the kitchen?
The kitchen at Flashback, with our time clock on the left: it kept drag time.

DARRIN HAGEN

Lindee suggested I take her place.

There are moments you remember all your life.

When I performed in Lulu's shoes that night (literally), I knew nothing would ever be the same again. Lindee did my makeup at the salon, I wore Mrs. K.'s white shimmy-fringe dress, I performed for a sophisticated fashion crowd and they loved me. I was Jazz-Baby-Cocktail-Hour-Gin-Flavored Fabulous as I worked the ramp to the strains of "Chicago":

I'm gonna be a celebrity. That means: somebody everyone knows / They're gonna recognize my eyes, my legs, my teeth, my boobs, my nose.

I spent the night partying with some cute straight bartenders at Monroe's. A nineteen-year-old University hockey player told me I looked good enough to eat, and bought me Grand Marnier all night.

The next day, at the hospital, I filled Lulu in on what a fabulous evening I'd had. Maybe if I'd been paying attention, I'd have noticed the cloud of sadness behind her words of encouragement.

A crucial moment in a mother's life is when her first child stops needing her help to walk.

Lulu got out of the hospital just in time for the first campaign show. She stepped on stage in a full length gown to hide the bandages. She never wore a backless gown again.

The crowd cheered, delirious with delight at her bravado, her circumstances, her timing. Her new appointment as Entertainer Of The Year merely strengthened her position. Her competitor, Lori St. John, didn't stand a chance. You could just tell that it was Lulu's turn.

Mary Mess' ball theme was "Breakfast at Tiffany's". To most, that meant jewelry. To me it meant wearing a large plastic fried egg on my head, woven into my Mz. Flashback crown. (Some people wear them on the inside, and some people wear them on the outside.) Mr. K. and I performed Sonny & Cher again, but the midget didn't show up, so it wasn't really as fun. By 11:00, Mr. K had become Mrs. K. after a quick trip to his hotel room, and did his Empress Walk, and then hurried upstairs and got out of makeup and into black drag for her Command Performance. Mega costume changes are mandatory.

It wasn't much of a contest that year. Lulu won effortlessly. She was crowned Empress IX at the Holiday Inn. The ballroom erupted with a roar of approval when the results of the voting were announced. She entered, the spotlight hit her, her beaded gown lit up the sky. She beamed radiantly, like a monarch gazing with love at her children, her people.

Lulu

The crowd leapt to their feet. The crown was placed on her head. It looked like it had always belonged there.

Outside the Holiday Inn, the hookers, not all of them women, stood on the corner of boredom and desperation, unaware that inside, one of their own had transcended all that pain and reached the top. They bent down to look in the windows of the cruising station wagons, the sedans on the hunt. Some cars slowed down and some sped up and each got a wink or a finger and some came round again and some gave up. But no one stopped.

At the Victory Brunch the next day, Lulu broke with tradition, and instead of promoting Lori St. John, she appointed me her Imperial Princess. Second in line to the throne.

We had arrived. There would be no turning back.

And to the victor go the Girls. We were suddenly surrounded by queens eager to share the edges of that spotlight, as they simultaneously plotted to wear the crown next. Lulu started selecting her court from among the intriguers, as a stirring of Motherly instinct tugged at my cotton gusset. I was halfway through my year, and it was time to start thinking

DARRIN HAGEN

about finding a successor, someone who would let us retain control. I took an interest in a fascinating work in progress. I was ready for my first child.

Tallulah.

Tallulah's campaign poster

DARRIN HAGEN

Giving Birth Is A Messy Experience

1985

"Sugar and spice and tits filled with rice...
that's what little boy/girls are made of."
                                              –Gloria Hole

For Tallulah life was full of firsts. An Italian Tundra Fairy from the word go, she had missed out on some fairly commonplace rites of passage for Canadian teenagers: driver's licenses, school dances, horseback riding, bowling.

Growing up blind can't be easy. Growing up a blind epileptic overweight homo in Canada's North, next to impossible.

Yet, there she stood; jaw and cheekbones sharp enough to slice bagels, eyes painted a la silent movie star, a Cleopatra wig framing her face.

Dom Fatale. Leather mini. Black fishnets always always always. Film noire seductress as new wave 80s hooker. Uneasy but strikingly easy.

She had designer friends. She wore designer clothes. She was designer drag.

Shiseido beard cover. Need I say more?

When Tallulah hit the stage, a life of cruel coincidence changed, finally, to a hope-filled Cinderella-type existence where dreams suddenly became possible. He who had never dared became She who never flinched: ten nails, two stilettos, and one Attitude. Her unique circumstances, and her general disdain of the tired drag we were trying to eliminate, made her a natural choice for inclusion into The Family.

I began tailoring her as the natural successor to my crown.

The end of my reign was a few months away. Tallulah and I started performing together, creating demented events like the Value Village fashion show, but she was an uneasy comic. She eventually found her style: slut with an attitude. The crowd loved it. Then, something happened that every drag queen had been hoping for since the early seventies:

Tina Turner made a comeback.

Some careers are built on accidents of timing. Tina's comeback sent every queen in town racing for their long brown wigs and teasing combs. Tallulah beat them all to the stage, and claimed it for herself.

Thus a Diva was born.

We still had to talk her into running for the crown. It took about a month of promising that all she would have to do would be to show up and be fabulous before she finally relented and said yes.

I breathed a sigh of relief. I could now focus on Stepping Down, confident that the next phase of the Dynasty was in place. Assuming Tallulah won.

Flashback. 1985, May long weekend. And I thought winning the crown was exhausting. Giving it away was worse. And, as luck would have it, my real family reentered my life at the height of the madness.

A cousin was getting married. I was to play piano at her wedding. Of course, it was on the night of my Command Performance. My parents, in town for the wedding, knew better than to ask to stay with me, but they had been asking questions about my workplace. I deftly dodged their inquiries by vaguely alluding to a "show" I had to do later.

I arrived at Flashback wearing a suit. The wedding reception had run overtime, and I was way behind schedule. The rest of the girls were in drag, waiting impatiently. The club was packed. I sat at the front of the stage with Mr. K. and we both lifted our glasses high, and the show began. We were the New Guard. And we flaunted it that night as The Family took to the stage: Lulu, our sister Floratron from Cowtown, Twiggy (my new aunt), Neon, Trash, and of course the candidates, our future, Dorky and Tallulah.

Dorky and Tallulah were running as a team for the Mr. and

Mz. title. Dorky was rapidly gaining visibility as the ultimate go-go boy. Night after night would find him in full view on the dance floor, dancing alone, a bright scarf jumping from hand to hand, lips turning blue from poppers. He often strolled through Flashback with Fluffy, a stuffed beagle that was more famous than any of us. Fluffy would follow Dorky through the mob, twelve feet behind his master, on a bright orange plastic leash. The crowd loved Fluffy. They would greet him as Dorky dragged him along the dance floor.

Fluffy ruled.

Tallulah seemed pretty much a shoo-in, but these things were never a sure thing. Her competition was Tinoir, a stunning tall black queen. Tallulah had more stage experience, but Tinoir had a knock-out figure and looked much more convincing in drag. All week, the two performed, dragging out all their sure-fire finery, hungry for the win.

It was still anyone's game.

We partied pretty hard that night. After the club closed, Lulu and Flora, still in drag, were holding Amii L. Nitrate upside

Tallulah and Gloria hold court
after the "Women in Rock" show, 1987

down on the bar with the booze pouring straight down her throat, while Neon, Dorky and I guzzled Schnapps and threw the shooter glasses against Gracie's mural. As we sat in the darkened club after hours, one of Tinoir's campaign posters burst into flames. We all stopped in mid-chug and watched it burn.

We took it as an omen of Tallulah's impending conquest.

Then all I remember is holding on to a bench, trying not to fall off the planet. Sometime in the night, Lulu and Flora left, and I found my way to a toilet and dry heaved for a couple of hours. Holding on to that toilet, the cold porcelain against my forehead, still in my suit on the filthy floor, I made a drunken mental note to give Millie shit for not scrubbing underneath the toilets.

Then all I remember is ... Gloria *en repos* in the drag room
(Iona's poem, written on the locker, says in part:
*...for somehow, in the irrevocable past,
is my head with that same brick wall: smash, smash, smash...*)

When Millie arrived to clean the club, the front door was wide open. She ventured inside warily. Broken glass, lights on, music still playing. Other than that, nothing seemed out of order. She made coffee, sat down and lit an Export A with a trembling hand. She thought back to nine years ago when she herself had come to the end of her year in the spotlight. As her last act from the throne, she had refused to pass on the crown. The fledgling club had been forced to scrape together the cash for a second crown.

She smiled. Then she wondered what happened to that crown...that all seemed like a lifetime away.

Finally she got up, filled a bucket and headed to the men's can. Then she screamed.

A pair of legs protruded from under one of the cubicles.

My legs.

Her scream woke me up. My suit was covered in chewing gum and god-knows-what-else. As I struggled to remember the night before, it gradually dawned on me that I had to crown the new Mz. that night. I was looking at a fourteen hour day, half of it in drag, and I was waking up in broad daylight around a toilet in a fag bar men's room with no idea what time it was.

I stumbled to action. *Those bitches deserted me!* I realized. Then, as I called a cab, Millie's scream rang out once more.

On her way through the drag room in the dark, Millie had tripped over a body.

It was Neon. Still dressed as Divine, half her faced smudged on the drag room carpet, cuddled up to our stage dummy, both blanketed in pink fun fur.

As Neon and I returned home in the taxi, I was fuming. The cabbie stared covertly into the mirror, probably watching for early signs of nausea. The sunlight burned through the windshield, Neon slumped against the window of the cab, her makeup leaving a huge streak on the glass. We drove past churchgoers on the way to worship; they stared at us as the cab drove by. Once at the apartment, I got even more hysterical. There was no place to sleep; drag queens lay everywhere, and Lulu and Flora had stolen my bed. Neon fell asleep on the floor. I took a shower, grabbed my drag bag, tiara and stepping-down gown, and headed back to the club to prepare for the Drag Races.

The Drag Races did not involve high-speed cars. They were more like a Crossdresser's Olympics.

Every May long weekend, Flashback prepared for the onslaught of madness. Before the Step-down, before the Crowning, before the queens painted, the staff would arrive, clean the club, warm up the barbecue, and fill up the dunk tank. The alley was blocked off at both ends. The beer cooler was stuffed with wading pools full of lime Jello, and I was going over the list of events for the day:

Tug-of War, Wet T-Shirt, Wet Jockstrap, Skiing for Five, Run Like a Girl/Boy, Waitress Races, Pie Eating Contests, Condom Blowup, Jello Wrestling (later it became Creamed Corn Wrestling), The Foxy Lady Rhinestone Turkey Baster Relay Marathon, The Squeeze-a-Snack Relay Marathon, The DQ Dunk Tank, The Lady Di Faint-A-Like Contest, and of course, The Drag Races, which involved running back and forth in the deep gravel in the alley, gradually layering on women's clothing from the Drag Pit. Naturally, maximum liquor intake was mandatory.

I poured a huge Tanqueray and supervised production. Once satisfied that everything was under control, I went into the men's can and performed the Big Shave. On a day this tightly scheduled, one had to plan ahead.

Then I counted the votes. Voting had occurred two nights earlier. The ballots were sealed in the office credenza, and nobody knew for the weekend who would win. I watched as Tallulah pulled ahead, then fell behind Tinoir. Unfolding and tallying the crumpled drunken ballots, I gradually saw The Family pull into a comfortable, then an unbeatable lead.

We had done it. My daughter would receive the Crown.

I pictured the moment when I would pin the Crown into her wig. My bosom swelled with motherly pride as I imagined it.

People were now arriving at the club. The alley was gradually filling up with buffed boys in obscenely short cut-offs, loud queens from Edmonton and Calgary, dykes in muscle shirts, and the crowd of fans that populated every drag event. Dance music blasted into the alley, and people streamed in and out of the club, carrying booze in plastic cups. Now and then a civilian would walk by, peer into the alley, and walk away with a confused look on his face. Or a Chinese family of eight would stop and watch for an hour, commenting to each other and laughing. Rhoda B., the essential Drag Races Emcee, was screaming into a microphone, cajoling people into entering events with strings of insults, bribes and threats.

Lulu and Flora arrived with Neon. Their hangovers could only be described as epic. They ordered drinks and we got all the rhinestone jewelry for the show together and ran it through the dishwasher. Millie stood with the other Dowagers (has-beens), avoiding direct sunlight. She was already drunk, even at this early hour, and was laughing and telling everybody how she had found me this morning. Tallulah and Dorky showed up, their nerves frazzled. I wanted so badly to tell them they had won, so they could relax and have fun with no pressure. Then I remembered how it felt when they called my name, a year ago, and decided that a little mental torment would build character. They mingled.

Bianca Bang-Bang getting ready for the drag races

Just as the Wet Jockstrap contest started, there was a phone call for me in the office.

My parents. "We were looking for the bar you work at, but all we could find at that address was an alley full of...well, I'm not sure..." Mom's voice trailed off.

I froze. They were at the phone booth down the street. No escape.

Mom and Dad's first view of the people I worked with was a bunch of pretty boys in jockstraps being hosed down, goose bumps raising, testicles shrinking, while drunken fags screamed with delight. I quickly led them inside and got them a beer. They stood and watched the mayhem, an expression of disbelief on their faces.

I realized the only thing connecting our two worlds at the moment was the river that ran between their home and mine.

How could I explain that I didn't really want them to see this? How to explain the importance of this day for me, the metamorphosis of me into a respected dowager, the year of change and growth that I had just passed through?

How to explain that this was a Family moment? My triumph, my journey was nearly complete, and I couldn't find the words to explain to them what they were seeing? Until this period of change was over, I couldn't afford to have them invade my new world.

How do you tell your family that they don't belong in this picture?

Mom and Dad were polite. They made conversation with a few of the gang, but they left after they were done their beer, without saying much. I watched them leave with relief. My attention, until now divided, returned to the task at hand.

Now I was behind schedule. Lulu and Tallulah were already painting in the Drag Pit. I joined them. Outside, the mayhem continued, as the queens prepared to dazzle indoors.

The actual show is a bit of a blur; too many hallucinogens, no doubt. All I really remember is my final performance as Mz. Flashback.

Every queen develops a repertoire over time. You try many things, and sometimes they don't pan out. When you find an act that makes the audience giddy with delight, you milk it for all it's worth. And one of my performances had quickly become legend Underground. This was "My Life".

A drag standard from the Shirley Bassey live recording, the song was about affirmation of values, strength of conviction, singleness of purpose, defying naysayers and forging your own road.

In my hands, it became a commercial for Life Brand cereal.

Picture a glam Vegas-style apparition in a floorlength gown, belting as only Bassey can, recorded applause thundering approval with every emotional crest of the music. Now add a giant bowl of breakfast cereal in milk, and watch the fun begin.

In my short career so far, it had become a trademark performance, and my one and only consent to the Glamification of Gloria.

The audience, as always, recognized the music immediately. (They usually knew the lyrics as well as we did.) I sat on a chair, delivering meaningful, pensive glances with mock seriousness. Then, at a pre-arranged cue, Lulu entered with a giant punchbowl and set it in my lap. I continued emoting. Lulu re-entered with a box of Life cereal just as I hit the chorus. She poured it into the bowl, then added a gallon of milk. There I sat in my custom-made gown, banner across my foamies, crown in my hair, with a sloshy bowl of what was rapidly becoming porridge in my lap. The music crested to its big finish, the orchestra punched the final chords, and the audiences, both canned and live, erupted with approval.

I sat soaking up the applause. This was the moment I had been waiting for all year: the spotlight cascading down, a stunning outfit, an amazing crowd drunk with delight as they bid me farewell. And of course, a video camera filming the entire spectacle, preserving this glorious moment forever.

Millie approached the stage. The first Mz. Flashback and the current Mz. Flashback on-stage together: the Past meets the Present to greet the Future. She stood next to me and leaned over to kiss me on the cheek.

The next few seconds replay in my mind like a scene from a bad horror movie. Millie reached down, lifted the punchbowl full of cereal and milk, and dumped it over my head.

A roar of laughter, then shocked silence, a gasp that still resounds in my ears, trapped on video for all time.

I sat frozen. My hair, coifed exquisitely, now hung in drippy tendrils. Droplets of milk sparkled in the spotlight. Little bits of porridgey wheat croutons clung to my crown, the very crown I was about to place on my daughter's head. My mascara ran down my cheeks in black teary lines, proving that "waterproof" on the label of something is as misleading as "one size fits all".

In my imagination, the doors all slam shut, the lights go out, and my telepathic rage wreaks havoc on everybody who has ever tormented or laughed at me.

By the time I came back to reality, Millie was gone, chased out of the club, and I was center stage with a fag bar full of people so quiet you could have heard an earring drop.

The proceedings came to a standstill while the stage was mopped. Someone threw a paisley bathrobe over my soggy shoulders. The crown was run through the dishwasher.

Tallulah's name was announced, and she hit the stage, glamorous, smile beaming bright enough to light up the Tundra. She took one look at me and burst out laughing.

After I pinned the Crown into her wig, she wouldn't even hug me. I was getting sticky.

Out in Tofield that night, I managed to get the Crown back. I climbed the pole in the chicken coop, and, knowing how afraid of heights she was, placed it on the very top.

Standing on the ground, I watched it as the sun rose. Once the sky was at its brightest, a shaft of sunlight collided with the big center rhinestone.

It shone like a star that had something to announce; an arrival.

A Birth.

I turned and joined Lulu and Ginger Snot in the outhouse. They were already writing the next chapter on the wall, giggling hysterically. Lulu turned to me. "Gloria, how do you spell placenta?"

A corny shot of Gretchen in 1991.
My cornfield, my photo credit...

Some Edmonton Queens (2)

Gloria and Twiggy in the drag pit

Ginger Snot

Gretchen Wilder in her
tampon swing dress

Zola and Cleo discovered at the end of the evening
that the pig's ears were real.

Iris in the drag room

DARRIN HAGEN

Armageddon
July 1, 1985

"I love a man in uniform...as long as he's got fifty bucks."
–Lulu LaRude

Flashback. The drag room. A long mirrored tunnel under the sound booth filled with skinny pasty boys. None of us *ever* saw the light of day. We were the boys who put the vamp in vampire. Sunlight touched us only when we rolled out of the bar at 10:00 am. The only colour in our cheeks was the stuff we painted on.

Lulu was stepping down as Entertainer of the Year. When she received the award we took it as a validation of our style of drag. We were now recognized as the New Wave. The old guard gave up trying to stop the revolution and embraced our innovations with a smirk of distaste, not realizing that the award would now remain in The Family for years to come. Who received the glory next was entirely up to Lulu.

And she wasn't talking.

Who would she choose? We were all in the running. Tallulah? Twiggy? Me? I was the main contender. And her best friend. And her roommate, but the roommate politics could work against me.

The show is already an hour late. Out in the bar, nobody notices.

Nerves frazzle on contact. It's a big night. All are applying makeup. Fanning lashes to dry the glue. Slipping on pair after pair after pair of nylons. In the hair spray-face-powder-perfume-cigarette-smoke-body-odor-choked air, curses and giggles and boyisms and girlisms bounce off the makeup mirror. Queens are mean, but before they take it out on you, they warm up on each other.

Iris, Kim Burly, John Reed (owner of Flashback) and Gloria
in the Flashback kitchen

Tallulah was a changed queen. Unafraid, the boy who had to be talked onto the stage had become gutsy, daring, and original. She had a crown now. The pressure to impress meant you worked harder, danced faster, went the extra mile. This pageant was her first important showcase since winning.

She was doing Grace Jones for the first time.

Watching a five-foot-ten Italian boy transform into an avante-garde Amazon Negresse takes some imagination in the early phases.

First: Erase the face. Glue painted over the brows. Avocado beard cover. (Tallulah was Italian. Three words: one o'clock shadow.) Then a deep brown base. Now of course, when you do cross-racial crossdressing (in the old days it was just called black chick drag) every piece of exposed skin has to be darkened. For Tallulah's debut as the disco diva : a sequin tube top. And leather micro mini. And little leather glovettes. This meant shoulders, back, armpits, face, neck, ears and midriff all had to be painted. Tallulah was behind schedule. And crabby.

Iris floats in. Late. Lulu bitches at her because it's her show and she can, and Iris always kind of inspires that kind of abuse. We call her Virus.

Iris was an artist who never quite got the hang of doing

drag. Not to be confused with a drag queen who never quite got the hang of being an artist. They're at least pretty. Sometimes.

There's no room for Iris at the head mirror and we don't really want her there so we send her back to get ready by the janitor sink we all pee in before the show. Definitely B-list.

Twiggy arrives. Also late, but we like her. She had turned out to be not just a worthy opponent, but definite Hole Family material. She was adopted as a sister of Lulu. Twiggy needed no mother, as there wasn't a lot you could teach someone like that. Slender, sophisticated, sparkly, our star dancer. She does things in heels that no woman would dare. Ex-Arthur Murray dance instructor reborn as Judy Garland's only talented daughter. *Not* Liza. We make room at the head mirror. Definitely A-list.

Tallulah's finally covered in black base so she gets ready to draw eyebrows. Then she realizes that her hands are already covered in the stuff, meaning everything she touches will be covered in brown smudges. Clothes, makeup, everything. She lights a cigarette to calm down.

The show is now two hours late. Out in the bar, nobody notices.

Gretchen, and Twiggy in boy drag, in the drag room

Neon in the drag room.

Twiggy's gossiping about Iris. Turns out when Iris' roommate, Lori St. John, was in the hospital, Iris pawned off all the furniture, appliances, even the fish tank. None of which belonged to her. She was probably wearing the profits right now in the form of that new beaded disaster of a gown she arrived in, illustrating once more that taste and price don't always travel together.

This amuses all of us greatly, except Tallulah who's just in a pissy mood. She heads to the janitor sink to wash her hands. Twiggy prances out for a shooter at the bar. Tallulah storms back in a rage because Iris won't move to let her clean up. Then the door flies open and Twiggy appears with a wild panicked look and is about to say something, some kind of warning, when she trips on her marabou cape and plunges in a sparkling heap to the foot of the stairs. We all jump up and run to her. We form a circle to pick her up and get her to a chair. Her ankle is fucked.

Just as we heave–the door opens again and two police officers step into the drag pit.

The room falls completely silent except for the subtle crinkle of plastic as someone discreetly tucks a bag of pot into a bra. Eight queens in various states of readiness, most in nothing more than pantyhose and dance belts, almost all with some kind of outstanding warrant, look up at them.

Lori St. John

The cops scan the room. The walls are covered in graffiti, Diana Ross posters, headdresses and autographs. The eyes looking back at them are heavy, dark, harshly powdered. You can never wear too much Bridget Bardot Black.

DARRIN HAGEN

Someone makes a "yummy yummy" kind of predatory noise at the back of her throat. It's for cop #2, a strapping tall young blond demigod in uniform. Lulu lights up a cigarette, squeezes a breast into shape and strikes a pose.

"Well, if it isn't the husbands. Whatcha lookin' for, boys?" She exhales into the already smoky air and steps up to them, all seven feet and two hundred plus pounds of her. She towers over both of them, completely filling the space between floor and ceiling. She gazes down at the older cop's bald spot.

In his best official unflustered voice, cop #1, an older married seen-it-all kind of guy says "We're looking for a Mister..." and then he says a man's name.

Understand, for a moment, that in the drag world, boy names just never came up. We had spent years as Twiggy, Gloria, Lulu, Tallulah. It's all we knew. So it took a moment to register.

Then a collective rush of realization: They were looking for Iris.

Everyone goes on naïve mode. We've got the home advantage. We know that even if Iris walks into the room, she's in drag. They won't recognize her—unless someone tells.

It's an interestingly powerful position to be in. We could pull the wool over the eyes of Edmonton's finest. That would be cool. Or we could send Iris off to spend the night in jail. In drag.

Also cool.

And just as we all sit pondering what not to say, Tallulah, for whom tact was rarely considered, screamed "Virus, there's some visitors here for you."

There's something titillating about watching a lanky blond cop handcuff a drag queen. Even when it's Iris. There, but for the Grace of God...

Iris didn't do the show that night. She spent the next twelve hours in a holding cell in full gear. Not an experience for the faint of heart. The lighting is merciless and by the time you're processed, your beard is growing through.

Or, at least, that's what I've heard.

Twiggy did do the show that night. Fucked ankle and all. She changed into something floorlength, we carried her to center stage and she did a Streisand stand-and-quiver kind of performance. The audience cheered, she bowed, and we carried her off.

Cleo in boy drag, and Justine, in the drag room

Tallulah didn't do the show that night. By this time she was so far behind schedule and so stressed out that none of us should have been surprised when her epileptic seizure started. At the mirror she dropped her black liner, her hand started to vibrate, then her arm spasmed and she fell back in her chair, pulling the makeup counter over on her way down. She's on the floor in a pile of tackle boxes and colour palettes, doin' the old *grand mal*.

The six remaining queens start screaming and running around. Red Cross didn't teach blending, so none of us went.

Finally, a doctor in full leather gear came in to help. An hour later she was driven home wrapped in a bathrobe. Still black. She slept for two days and then woke up. Not black. Her bedding, however, was a different story. She didn't remember a thing.

The first thing she asked me was whether or not she had won.

I had to tell her Lulu had given me Entertainer of the Year that night.

Tallulah was furious. She had wanted that one badly. But after a four hour fight, we ordered pizza and made up. I also promised her I would give her the title when I stepped down. I had that kind of Power now.

Life with Lulu had become exclusive. We literally spent

every second of every day together, planning shows, plotting schemes, deciding who would be the next Superstar, grooming successors. But often, we would argue about the other's choices. She was still perceived as the leader in most circles, despite the fact that I was officially the boss on the stage we all lived to perform on.

Lulu didn't know it yet, but by naming me her successor she had just committed the biggest mistake of her drag career. I had two crowns now. We were even once more.

The music from that performance still rings in my ears.

Oh, she looked so good,
Oh, she looked so fine.
And I got this crazy feelin'
That I'll make her mine, make her mine, make her mine:
G-L-O-R-I-A
Tower bells chime
Ding dong they chime
I said that Jesus died for somebody's sins
But not mine.

As I performed that night, hoping against hope that I would win, flipping my hair around, trying out my more serious, sexy side, I was already dreaming of the day when I didn't have to share that spotlight with anyone.

Despite all the chaos backstage, we all performed our asses off that night. The show ended up going on three and a half hours late, but it was a drag show.

Nobody noticed.

Tallulah was a changed queen...

Two Men Enter—
One Man Leave
September, 1985

"It's all fun until someone smudges an eyebrow."
–Tallulah

Lulu stepped down as Empress a few months later. It was the Ball of the decade (literally; the Tenth Year of Glamour had begun). The theme was 'Let Them Eat Cake', and our first entrance was as The Royal Wedding Party, with Lulu as the blushing bride, and Tallulah, Twiggy and I as her bevy of virgins-in-waiting. To make things unusual, I wore a walkman and listened to my own music as we performed "Goin' to the Chapel/Boogie Woogie Bugle Boy". As Imperial Princess, I stood next to my Dragmother on the dais all night, receiving out-of-town dignitaries, watching as platitudes and gifts were showered at Lulu's feet, mopping her brow to preserve her makeup till her Final Walk.

The candidates for Empress were Amii L. Nitrate and Lori St. John, fresh out of the hospital minus part of a leg, back for another challenge. Lori's diabetes had landed her in surgery to amputate a foot. She simply switched to flats and moved on.

Ball weekend. It was what we lived for.

Picture two or three floors of a downtown hotel, the Holiday Inn again in this case, packed with room after room of men with far too much luggage, tweezed eyebrows, garment bags and loud voices, bustling from suite to suite to "borrow" drag essentials, share beauty tips and drug connections, and basically crank 'til they drop. The Empress is the star of the entire week.

The big ballroom is decorated, multiple spotlights in place, video cameras poised to catch the proceedings. At one end of the ballroom stands the dais, on a dramatically lit stage, with two thrones and some extra seating for the prince and princess, along with some celebrity out-of-town dignitaries. A long runway extends from the dais down the middle of the ballroom, with tables surrounding it Las Vegas style.

The Ball is part ritual, part fashion show. The Empress is part politician, part photo opportunity.

Being the most fabulous was the entire name of the game.

There was a fair amount at stake, too. Canada was currently run by the youngest Empresses on record. Lulu, Calgary's Floratron and Vancouver's Christopher Peterson were a mere twenty years old when they ascended the throne. This Western Canadian Triad was knocking the American Empesses out of the way, receiving standing ovations at all the Balls south of the border. We had something to prove. We were young and adventurous. And thin.

A large number of Americans were at Lulu's Ball. She had made quite an impression in cities like Spokane and Seattle, and the Empress club responded by travelling north, where the Big Onion queens were rapidly developing a reputation as the wildest party children of all Canada.

The Ball started late, naturally, but by the middle of the first

Tallulah

set of Entrances, the ballroom was packed. The lobby of the hotel was filled with curious onlookers as the Queens strutted their stuff. The elevator doors opened, and impossibly large creatures emerged, grandly sweeping across the floor towards the ballroom. The air filled with the shrieks of adoration as mutual compliment trading occured, everyone's voice acquiring an epic tone of hysteria, as befits an occasion of such majesty. Every *ding* of the elevator signalled another flood of taffeta-rhinestone-hairspray creations, until the entire main floor was submerged in headdresses and leather and capes and crowns.

Even Millie was coming out of a four-year hiatus and donning a frock for the event.

The Big Buzz of the evening, however, was Tallulah.

The Flashback Entrance at any Ball was one of the highlights of the evening. Everyone knew what Tallulah was planning: Thunderdome had recently hit the theaters, and we had all seen the video. A post-apocalyptic Tina Turner stood against a

Tallulah: *"We don't need another hero..."*

fiery smoky sky, encased in futuristic chain-mail mesh, belting "We Don't Need Another Hero." Tallulah had the dress copied, and the ballroom sat in breathless anticipation. Then, the unthinkable happened: minutes before Tallulah was scheduled to hit the ramp, we heard her music start.

Lulu and I looked at each other in horror. Repeat drag numbers at a ball were fairly common until we came along; but this was a Family moment, and some Empress from Spokane was stealing our thunder. Lulu froze with a smile on her face (she had to be polite), and I just stared at the stage.

Out in the lobby, the elevator opened and Tallulah stepped out. She heard her music coming from the ballroom, and a moment of panic as she assumed it was hers. She ran to the entrance and saw her number being done by somebody else.

The old Tallulah would have taken one look at the ballroom, turned on her heel and fled back to her hotel room.

But this was a queen with a crown now. One look in the full-length mirror in the lobby confirmed it.

The music in the ballroom ended to polite garden applause. A tepid response at best. Then, immediately after, the song started again. Tallulah stepped into the ballroom.

The audience leapt to its feet.

Tallulah was a reincarnation of Tina's Thunderdome character. Silver metal mesh draped off her shoulders, reinforced with armored bra, silver gloves, and a platinum mohawk crowning her head, then cascading down her back.

She stood in the double spotlights and fireflies of light flew off her frame and shimmered on the walls of the Ballroom. With every chorus, her silver fist shot into the air in a gesture of defiance.

Goose bumps.

On the dais, Lulu and I looked at each other and smiled.

Amii L. Nitrate became Empress X. We would all soon be sorry. Poor Lori St. John retreated again into obscurity. She would have to find another way to make her mark on the world.

Amii lasted a few months as Empress, then cracked from the pressure, abdicated, and moved to Saskatchewan, where she opened a hair salon and ran for Empress again eventually. It was a rocky shift of decade, and no one could have anticipated what happened next.

The crown was passed to Mother Jean, an eighty-year-old woman who had been a fixture in the Underground since the days of Millicent. She was, and is still, the only woman to wear the Big Onion Crown.

There is much that could be said about the age-old relationship between a straight woman and a gay man. Intensify all of that, and you might understand the connection between some straight women and drag queens.

Mother Jean was a dear friend of Millie's in year one. Because of her constant emotional support through the years and her tireless vigilance for respect for the drag community, she was given the title Imperial Gay Mother Of All Alberta. She brought a lot of dignity to the throne that year. She was the proudest Empress Regent that there could have possibly been.

She could also pack away more rye than any of us on a given night.

Millie with Imperial Gay Mother of All Alberta, Mother Jean

Gloria explores performance art, 1986

DARRIN HAGEN

Little House On The Prairie
1984-1986
11415-100 ave.

"A Queen's home is her closet."
–Gloria Hole

o truly understand a species, find out where it lives. A drag house is an easy one to spot. It will be a large prominent structure. Corner lot, probably with a dramatic entrance or turret or balcony or something fabulous about it.

Chances are, if it looks like a scene from a costume epic could be filmed in the yard, it's rented by queens.

Never just one. Always a group. Usually about the same age, philosophy and build. If all the queens were the same size, you could quadruple your drag wardrobe.

When Trash approached us one day and said that she had found the most amazing house and would we move in with her, we shrieked with delight. Lulu and I teamed up with Trash to become the founding Mothers of Walla Walla West. Within a year, the address could make a cabby quake with fear.

Lulu and I packed our things, said good-bye to Annie Hole and Joolz, and headed to the new house. The first load of junque filled the big green van. The piano was loaded into the back of a truck, with me fretting over it, sitting by its side. Lulu held on the other side. She talked me into playing something while we drove. I launched into "Cry Me A River", and Lulu sang into the rhinestone turkey baster with a white feather boa flapping in the wind.

No stage was too small, especially if it was on wheels.

Who moved in next depended on what we needed most. The population of Walla Walla West swelled at times from five

Ora rests after a tough night

to eleven queens, depending on who Lulu was feuding with, or how close Ball Weekend was. As the ruling queens, we hosted most of the out-of-town Empresses when they visited.

We invited a post-apocalyptic punk poet queen named 𝕁ona 𝔹ox, and Prickles, an ex-queen with a drinking problem, to join us. They seemed to balance things quite nicely. Iona immediately insisted that we take down all the porcelain Pierrot clowns that Lulu collected. Iona had a phobia about clowns: they gave her nightmares. She had never been to a McDonald's for that very reason.

When Iona unpacked, we saw a baby's headstone among her things.

We didn't ask.

The future seemed a million spotlight years away, but Lulu had hers all figured out. "When I'm sixty-five I'm getting a sex change, 'cause everyone hates a dirty old man, but everyone loves a dirty old woman."

During the week, things were fairly normal. We worked our various waitress jobs, hung out at the bar, even had a bit of a day schedule. Lulu and I would take the bus to work on cold mornings, watch all the normal people scurrying to their normal jobs in their normal clothes, and wonder where we fit into the grand scheme of things. Looking around, it was easy to believe we were all aliens, like Iona said. There weren't a lot of people like us, it seemed.

Then on the bus one morning, Lulu nudged me. "There!" she said excitedly, "There we are! That's us!" I looked.

Two ancient old ladies stood on the corner. One was nearly blind, the other curved over until she was half her size. They held onto each other as they crossed the street, achingly slow, each trusting the other to guide or support. The world rushed past them while they lived frozen in time, like two ancient sisters dressed for presentation. Or preservation.

Alone in the world.

But we were never alone on the weekend. The neighbors could usually hear the hum of activity on a Saturday morning. Bette Midler's "Live at Last" double album would waft on clouds of marijuana smoke into the alley at the crack of noon. It was required learning for every queen–memorize every joke and song. As the day wore on, boys would start arriving on foot or by cab, carrying wigheads, bags of pantyhose, or dresses that blinded you in the sunlight.

The living room became the Follies rehearsal hall. Move the couch and coffee table to one side and work it, girls. In one afternoon we could choreograph the opening and closing production numbers. By the end of it, all are exhausted and sweaty, sitting around in stubble and pumps, listening to the same song over and over and over, lip-synching quietly to themselves and smoking.

Then–the painting began.

For the neighbors, this ominous silence was a warning. Only one thing could require that kind of silent focus. One by one the wigs in the upstairs window would disappear.

It must have looked strange to the neighbors. Every Saturday, eight men would arrive. You would never see them leave.

Two or three cabs would pull up to the house, the front door would open and a parade of huge feathered shiny freaks would emerge, snake through the front yard

Iona Box

Iona had a phobia about clowns...

and cram itself into the taxis, trying not to crush, fold, bend or wrinkle anything. Not an easy task. The bigger the hair, the closer to God.

Then...hours of silence. The evening ticked by. The neighbors would go to bed.

At 5:00 am, an ungodly screech would slice through the night. It was usually Lulu announcing to the world that we were home, but it could have easily been Ora or Trash or Tina or Iona or Prickles or Neon or Reena or some out of town Empress or all at once. The house would explode with life and noise and punk rock and disco and occasionally a brawl or a person falling through a plate glass window. Flashback would empty its entire contents into our house. Skinheads and models and junkies and leather queens would head for Walla Walla West. Four floors of party ambience: the main floor had the keg of draft in the kitchen, the loudest music, a piano, lots of mannequins and unmatched lamps, and dozens of defunct telephones.

The second floor was bedrooms, each uniquely spectacular in its own disarray. The attic was like a huge drag fort. Trash held court here, supervising the wandering guests. The basement was usually where the hard-core druggies hung out.

Amityville.

And everywhere you looked on every floor–drag. We lived knee deep in it.

As real people would wake and look out of their windows, they would see a four-car taxi lineup in front of the house; a yard littered with unconscious bodies draped fetchingly; Prickles stumbling and mumbling into people, spilling flat beer wherever he went; Lulu on the back balcony in leopard sunglasses and a pink princess gown screaming hello to the sun. Iona would be reading snark poetry in the kitchen, and I would be upstairs working on my favourite blond boy.

Those were the days.

We were gradually turning drug use and partying into an art form. The menu from those days reads like a who's-who of stimulants: liquor, bennies, pot, acid, MDA, poppers, the occasional cocaine, speed, mescaline, nicotine, caffeine, sugar, sex, and of course, mushrooms. Our marijuana dealer lived two doors down, and many a morning would find one of us clad only in a bathrobe, tiptoeing down the street with a coffee cup in hand, needing to "borrow a cup of reefer".

One weekend at the bar, one of the managers gave us some mushrooms that had been confiscated from one of the patrons. If there was anything we appreciated, it was free narcotics. We decided to brew a pot of tea, thereby ensuring that everyone hanging with us that night would get some. We were poor, but generous. We partied all night, laughing and hallucinating. The mushrooms were some of the strongest I'd ever had; hours went by, morning came and we were still flying. Then Iona decided to go and buy cigarettes. She put on a stupid hat for effect, then stepped outside.

Seconds later, she was back, in a total panic. "The house is surrounded by cops!" she screamed, locking the door behind her.

We laughed, thinking she was just trying to be funny. Then Trash looked out the living room window. "Oh my God, she's right," she muttered.

We stopped laughing, then raced up to the attic, which had a full view of the street. Indeed, there were cops everywhere. But as we watched, we realized they weren't casing out the house. The police stood on guard

Some Edmonton Queens (3)

Tallulah, with Dorky Louise in a rare drag appearance

Dorky Louise, my only son

Gloria and Ora ready to terrorize the town

every half block, standing, staring straight ahead. As far as we could see, the neighborhood was fortified. But why?

We went downstairs and brewed more mushroom tea. Now that peril was no longer imminent, we could return to our plans. Then someone flipped on the television, and we saw the Pope landing in The Big Onion.

And the Basilica he was heading for was a mere three blocks from Walla Walla West.

We began selecting outfits for a Papal audience.

Nothing like a tiny act of defiance to get you through the day. Of course, we knew we wouldn't get to meet him. But how many chances do you get at freaking out *that* audience? And of course, we didn't do drag. We just wanted to dress like aliens and see how people would react. We finished our tea and headed out.

The Big Onion had done its best to prepare for the Pope. All along the Popemobile's route, graffiti had been painted over, walls decorated, reality prettied up, the surface of the city polished, denying the existence of anything ugly or obscene or deviant. All along Jasper Avenue, parade seating was set up, packed with anxious Catholics for hours before he arrived. Police stood on rooftops, armed. Heavily, it seemed. The air was thick with a deep, powerful authority, the sky rumbled and churned with clouds, and suddenly, being an obvious freak seemed dangerously close to public suicide. We surveyed the scene from the Mac's parking lot where Lulu and I had fought off the fagbashers, and we all removed our ladies' hats, cat-eye glasses and jewelry, and put them in our coat pockets.

This was definitely not the time.

"Keeping the faith certainly takes a lot of artillery," observed Iona.

"We can't see a thing from here. Let's go further down the street, and maybe we'll catch a look at the Popemobile," said Lulu. We moved past the street vendors hawking icons and souvenir Pope Plates, and eventually found a spot a few blocks down.

A hush fell over the crowd. Then the sky darkened, and we heard a helicopter approaching. It swooped down the street, roaring, clearing the way, followed by a rank of black motorcycles, some black cars, then finally...

The Popemobile sped into view, a plastic bubble in the back of a van with a little white man waving robotically, gone before the crowd could do anything but gasp and race after him.

We stood still as people ran past us excitedly. We may not have felt the faith, but we certainly felt the power.

But power with guns is easy.

We headed home. The police still stood facing the house, staring straight ahead with self-importance. We went inside, opened all the windows, and blasted drag music onto the street, and danced in the window where everyone could see.

And made more tea.

The first mouse made an appearance around then. We had a little war with that mouse, gradually wearing him down until Lulu actually caught him in a shoebox. The plan was to get it out of the house, but Lulu took one look and fell in love with it. Instead of putting him in the snow, she went two doors down to Le Marchand Mansion and let it go inside.

Eventually we destroyed the house. Not all at once, and not on purpose. It just kind of happened.

One day the kitchen wall fell in as Trash was doing the dishes. Just peeled away and collapsed. Dozens of mice were suddenly visible running through the woodwork. A winter storm blew my

Kim Burly tries the *avant-garde*

Ora and Gloria

bedroom window in one day. Immediately the whole upper floor plummeted to -30°[2]. It was weeks before I could afford to have it fixed. Lulu threatened to move somewhere warm if I didn't do something about it. I suggested Hell and stormed out for a week.

The strain was beginning to show. Prickles started doing bizarre stuff like moving all the dirty dishes from the kitchen to the upstairs bathroom and leaving them there. Iona's mother died in B.C., and suddenly Iona sank into a major depression. Trash was secretly planning to move out and go to Vancouver because she was a nomad and never really felt right owning so much stuff. Lulu was driving herself crazy meddling with the machinations of Drag Politics, and I couldn't escape the nagging feeling that there had to be more to life than chasing two-bit crowns. I wanted to make Art. And I wanted to be beautiful doing it. Lulu did her best to keep me doing comedy while she lived the role of the tragic diva.

The battle between Lulu and I for control of Edmonton's drag turf heated up after that. Fuck community. Fuck this. This was about us.

The seeds of discontent had been sown. The better I got at doing drag, the more I threatened her supremacy. Lulu had moved into the unenviable position of the queen to conquer. Her hold on an audience was hard to describe—possibly it had more to do with who she was offstage, but she left crowds cheering madly.

My Mentor. My Mother.

We had ruled as a team, but when Lulu and Gloria were spoken of, Lulu's name always came first, and I was starting to get bitter.

I was no longer suited for second in line to the throne, not just comedy relief anymore. Waist length red hair made me more vain than God. I learned sultry. I studied sexy. My routines reinvented sleaze. And, I learned that I had better legs than she did.

I told you I was bitter. Remember: there can only ever be *one* queen.

Lulu and I spent weeks not speaking to each other. The bills mounted. We ignored them. We had shows to do! How dare

---

[2] Celsius. At -40°, the two scales meet at frigid.

real life intervene? Queens moved in and out and back in, the drag piled higher and higher, only now there were mice burrowing through it.

The sheriff arrived to seize something for non-payment of rent, and the only thing worth taking was my piano. I called Mom in tears.

She wired me the rent. Lulu and I began making plans to move.

Then I fell in love. And nothing can tear two sisters apart faster than a man.

That was the end of Walla Walla West. We abandoned ship. In our wake we left behind furniture, tons of newspapers, clothes that didn't fit, broken appliances, dirty dishes, an eight-foot fig tree, a statue, a headstone, and the garbage from every queen that had ever lived there.

I took one last look at the living room before I locked the front door that final time.

It was already full of ghosts.

Lulu and I moved into an apartment, but the wheels were in motion. I started making plans to move again. But I didn't tell Lulu. Right down to the day I left, we didn't speak about being apart. The words didn't exist because what we had gone through together was too unique, too manic, too special for mere words.

When I saw her at the Club the next week, we didn't mention the The Big Move. We never did speak about it. But the Big Onion did. Queens gossiped about it for weeks, waiting for the explosion that, in spite of all the unspoken hurt, never happened.

Life went on.

That house is gone now.

So are a lot of the people who lived there.

Twiggy

Go Into The Light
1986-1987

"I'm no social butterfly; I'm a social moth."
—Twiggy

Sometimes a star is born in spite of herself. In the summer, the Big Onion explodes into four months of festivals, parties, events, and gatherings. Maybe winter in The Big Onion builds a little too much character. Maybe it has something to do with being sequestered in perpetual darkness for so many months.

Some people prefer that darkness to light, unless that light is a spotlight. Then that darkness is pierced with a dazzling ray of hope, enough to keep you drawn to its brilliance.

Twiggy was the Moth that couldn't stay away from the light.

Yet she lived in perpetual night. 4:00 a.m. would find her sucking back her eighth pot of coffee, chain-smoking and doodling gown designs on a placemat at whatever all-night restaurant hadn't gone bankrupt from her patronage. She would address the graveyard shift by name, and was often still doodling and requesting refills when the changing of the guard ushered in the morning.

Twiggy would often awake just in time to make it to the club for the peak of the evening. Her life was a constant race against the sun; the more she could squeeze into those precious hours of night, the better she would sleep when the sun finally came out.

The Underground was designed for people just like Twiggy. That's why she surprised me when she agreed to follow me to The Surface.

The reputation of The Hole Family had spread like a

brushfire across the Prairies. We were now The Old Guard; there was no getting around it. Once the alternative becomes mainstream, it's only a matter of time before there's a new alternative waiting in the wings to dethrone it.

Tallulah's year ended with one of the largest parties Flashback had seen. She was an audience favorite from the word go, one of those performers you wanted to see succeed. When she stepped down, there was never any question as to who would be next to wear the crown: Twiggy was redefining drag movement every time she hit the stage. She was fluid, graceful, charismatic and confident. In spite of herself.

Twiggy possessed a tragic flaw: she could sleep through anything.

Many a time we would struggle to wake her up for a rehearsal. She could sleep through the phone ringing two hundred times right next to her bed. She could sleep through queens jumping up and down on her bed. She could sleep through water being poured on her head. Many times we would just give up, assuming we would have to do the show without her.

She would show up seconds before the show started, plop herself into the running order, and wow the audience. Flawlessly, as if she had been rehearsing for weeks. Never missing a step.

Ya gotta hate a queen like that.

Ya gotta hate a queen like that...

She made every show she was in a better place to be. And as long as you didn't mind the occasional set of earrings disappearing, or your evening gloves vanishing before a performance, she could be a lot of fun, too.

Now, of course, "borrowing" things from each other was a common tool, useful

Neon

when drag shortages hit. There was nothing worse than getting halfway through your face and realizing you were out of powder. Thankfully, because we all got ready together, someone else could always float you through the crisis: however, it is easier to ask for forgiveness than for permission. So, often we would merely help ourselves to each other's stashes. It was an understanding that kept us all from killing each other.

Eventually, the club bought a set of lockers for the drag room. That settled things for a while, but anything left out in the open was communal drag property.

Twiggy's Mr. Flashback was only the second woman to possess the title, the first being a lesbian named Joey, back in the days of Millicent.

This woman was Neon, adopted into The Family when she traveled North to party for weekends, then weeks, then months at a time. Originally a member of the Calgary Del Rockos, she couldn't resist the lure of the Northern Lights, and eventually relocated permanently to the Big Onion.

Twiggy and Neon should have been Mr. & Mz. Flashback X, because 10 was the number they looked like when they stood next to each other. Twiggy was named for her slight, lithe

Twiggy

frame, while Neon became famous for impersonating all the "larger-than-life" women: Jennifer Holliday, Mama Cass, Divine; all without the aid of padded dresses.

Their reign could have been a stormy one, as both egos were larger than life. Neon, a drag queen trapped in a woman's body, had been performing with crossdressing troupes from the second she was old enough to step foot in a fag bar; Twiggy was a Diva from the word go. Their competitive nature meant they drove each other to new heights, each vying for the lioness' share of the spotlight.

It made for a fireworks kind of year.

I broke my promise to Tallulah and gave Twiggy Entertainer of the Year.

Around then, we started exploring the Surface. We were getting too numerous to stay Underground forever. The fag bar was fun, but straight people freaked when we performed for them. A few professional gigs and the occasional mention in the papers started fueling The Dream: to go pro.

After weeks of thinking carefully, I applied to the Fringe Festival to do a drag show. I chose Twiggy to write the show with me, and asked every one of the queens to come along for the ride.

Every queen but Lulu.

Maybe I had a chip on my shoulder. Maybe I resented Lulu's continuing hold on the fans. Sometimes it all seemed way too easy for her.

Maybe I just had to do it without Mom.

I remember cruising down Whyte Avenue on the hood of a '57 Pontiac in my new mermaid outfit on the opening day of the Fringe. We had transcended "freak" status and entered "local oddity" territory. Twiggy and Neon were by my side, (the rest of the Girls refused to do drag that early in the day), and there was a palpable buzz of excitement in the air.

Once you go public, there's no turning back.

Guys in Disguise 1987
Back row: Kim Burly, Nellie Michael, Neon, Tallulah, Ora Fice
Front row: Gloria, Shanann, Twiggy

Boys Will Be Girls

August 1987

"Watch that first step...it;s a doozie."
–Lulu teaching me how to walk in heels

There's something scary about the Surface. First, it's way too bright. Underground dwellers usually squint as they see the sunlight for the first time.

Second, people dress a lot plainer.

Lastly, people on the Surface frighten easily. We figured that out quickly and turned it to our advantage.

In my wildest dreams, I never would have imagined causing anything more than a minor ripple on the surface of daylight in The Big Onion.

But this was The Fringe. And anything could happen at The Fringe.

Or at least, that's what I had been told.

I hadn't actually been to a Fringe. Living Underground, we found that the celebrations of summer often went unnoticed because of our hectic party schedule.

In the eighties, the most famous drag queen was Boy George. Divine was gaining respectability as an actor, and Ru Paul was years away from birth. The decision to go public was not one that came easy. Were the Prairies ready for the local crossdressers to display their wares? Could Alberta face its own dark side and face the drag music? Could they accept a part of their society that the majority was terrified of admitting even existed?

Or would we get beat up?

I had no answers as I filled out the application form. All I knew was that the time felt right.

But as soon as word got out, I began to wonder.

The Underground's reaction swung between vague words of encouragement and disbelief. No one could believe that straight people would line up and pay money to see an act that most fags considered, at best, passe, or, in the case of the militant queers, "reinforcing negative stereotypes of the gay community".

What they didn't realize was that it takes a real man to wear a dress on the prairies.

Twiggy and I would write the script, and all the girls with any talent would be in the show. That is, with the exception of Lulu.

Even as I say those words now, they seem harsh. But at the time, there was more than just friendship or sisterhood involved. Without Lulu, I could be sure that the control stayed in my hands.

I had been waiting for this all my life. But I knew that it wouldn't happen the way I wanted it to if Lulu was hanging over my head.

Twiggy, however, threw a whole new element of danger into the proceedings. Twiggy could sleep through her own funeral.

Mornings were usually spent trying to get Twiggy out of bed. I would start phoning her hours before we had to actually be anywhere. One of the most effective ways to get her out of bed was to phone, and once ringing was underway, put your own phone on hold and go get something done. Checking back every ten minutes or so, I would hear her line ring and ring and ring, then I'd go back to whatever it was I'd been doing.

Despite this, Twiggy and I wrote a play that summer. Actually, two plays. The first still languishes in my files, seventy hand-written pages of soap opera importance, with a murder, deceit, tragedy and guilt all woven together. The first read took two and a half hours. And we still wanted to do some drag numbers.

Everyone had pretty much been cast as themselves. The cast consisted of Twiggy, Tallulah, Kim Burly, Neon, Ora and myself. My high school friend Shanann was signed up to sing the original song. And we hired a queen wannabee, because we needed a boy for some of the numbers. His name was Nellie Michael, later to become Ginger Snapped.

The tales of rehearsals read like Macbeth. Not only were we

inexperienced, but drag queens arc notorious for making a bad scene worse. I may have thought I was a writer, but I was definitely not a director. We frantically collected dresses, painted sets, hoofed our way through hour after hour of choreography. The first script was tossed; Twiggy and I began writing another.

That's when mutiny began. Queen by queen, murmurs of dissent began to filter back to my panic-stricken ears.

First Ora tried to quit. She was actually running for Empress XII at the same time that all of this was happening. I pulled her aside and managed to convince her that a pro show would only enhance her campaign image.

Then Kim Burly started her schizophrenic routine. She was the reigning Mz. Flashback, and my second daughter. The strains of half-truths began to unravel the already tenuous threads holding us together. Kim Burly wanted out: she'd had enough, and wanted to return to just being a bar queen. The troupe we had created was tearing apart the Family. And the Underground community lurked nearby, ready to grab tales of confusion and run them to the doubters, the few who actually wished us ill because we were dragging the dirty drag laundry into the sunlight where everyone could see.

Time for decisive action. I did the only thing I knew I could get away with. We had an emergency meeting, and I

Cleo, Gloria and Tallulah

announced that if anyone pulled out this close to opening night, I would personally see to it that they never performed at Flashback again.

The girls looked at me. No one really believed that I could do that, but no one was willing to test that theory.

The two main dissenters, Ora and Kim Burly, shut up after that. If Ora won as Empress, she would need that stage for a whole year, and Kim Burly's hold on the Mz. Flashback crown was tenuous enough already; the management had already threatened to crown someone else if she didn't start showing up and doing something. The unique circumstances that led to this were actually fairly simple.

I had never stepped down.

Programming that stage was now my job. Ever since I had held the crown, I had supervised the grooming and coronation of the new Mz. Flashback, planned her year, did her posters, choreographed her shows, and made her look good. Tallulah had insisted on that: it was the only way we could convince her to run for the title. Twiggy and Neon had worked with me to create shows that were polished, unusual and very funny. Flashback was the drag capital of the world, according to us.

And Guys In Disguise, as we were now called, was billed as the In-House troupe of Flashback.

Around this time, we were faced with another serious discussion.

We had just finished a group photo shoot above Flashback in one of the studios that filled the rest of the building. As we piled into the freight elevator to go back downstairs, Ora said, "I want prints of those for my Empress poster."

"Girl, you'll be able to just clip it out of the paper!" I laughed. Tallulah looked at me suddenly. "Which paper?" she demanded.

"Probably the *Journal*, maybe the *Sun*, I don't know." I didn't see the problem.

"My mom reads the Journal," said Ora.

"Won't she be proud when she sees you in the paper."

Tallulah butted in. "With our real names in print?"

"Well, yeah, I mean, this is the real thing, right? We have to sell tickets. I want pictures of the whole gang in and out of costume."

"In the Journal?" Tallulah was getting crabby.

"What's the problem? I mean, we're queens. It's not like we live in a closet." Now I was getting crabby.

"Speak for yourself, Gloria. My whole family might see this," said Ora.

"You're running for Empress! This is not the time to be camera shy." I couldn't see the problem. "My family will see this, too. Everyone in Rocky Mountain House reads the *Journal*. But this is a legitimate theater event. And we're artists. I want people to know who we are."

Tallulah rolled her eyes. "You mean you want people to know who *you* are."

I stared at her. "This is for all of us," I said quietly. "Don't you want to be famous?"

"We're already famous enough for me," said Kim Burly. All she had ever wanted was to be Mz. Flashback. "This stopped being about us ages ago. I don't see why we have to out ourselves just because you've got something to prove."

We took a vote. Tallulah still held back, nervous about her family in Yellowknife. Then finally, she relented.

Guys UnDisguised: Neon, Gloria, Shanann, Kim Burly, Tallulah, Ora Fice, Twiggy, Nellie Michael (Ginger Snapped)

We did one more photo shoot: at the *Journal* building. The logistics of moving that many queens from place to place were just beginning to occur to us. It took two or three taxis, depending on how big the hair was that day. We piled out of a convoy of cabs, lamé flashing in the bright daylight. People waiting for buses stood staring as we entered the building. The eight of us strolled through the newsroom and you could have heard an eyelash drop. The photographer, dubious at first, brightened up when he saw us work the camera. We posed, minced and giggled our way to a drop-dead gorgeous group photo.

With all this publicity to do, who had time to rehearse?

We resumed panicking. In a hideous coincidence, the Fringe was opening on Ball weekend. Not only were we opening a show on the surface for the first time, but we all had our Underground duties to fulfill, as well. Ora was running for Empress, Kim Burly had a Flashback Entrance to put together, Twiggy and I each had Entertainer of the Year performances to consider. Plus, we had vowed not to use any of

Gloria 1987
stepping down as Entertainer of the Year

the numbers in our Fringe show in any other context, which meant coming up with new performances. The day of the Fringe parade, as we floated down Whyte Avenue on our way to respectability, we had already been awake for two days, buzzing on bennies to stay alert. After the parade, we took off our makeup, made coffee, sat for a couple of hours staring at nothing, then packed up our costumes and got started putting on makeup for the Ball. The whole weekend was such a blur, that the impact of what we'd done barely registered.

We opened Monday. At noon.

The scheduling Gods at the Fringe obviously had it in for us. For a drag queen, a noon show means prep starts at 7:00 a.m.

We sold out. No one was more surprised than us.

And the demographic of the audience surprised us; mostly straight, mostly female. We stumbled through our routines. The performance was our first real run of the whole thing. It felt like it lasted forever.

As we bowed, we received a respectable round of applause. But the show had problems.

That evening, we rebuilt the show. Top to bottom. Brand new show tapes were made. All the impersonations were cut. Tina Turner had bombed, as had my cherished Kate Bush performance. The only thing we could count on was comedy. So the whole show became about parading the shtick we had developed to entertain ourselves in the jaded Underground.

The reviews hit the next morning. Suddenly our faces were everywhere. In and out of drag. The parade had attracted a lot of attention, but nothing compared to the pre-show performances we started to give.

Our next show sold out as well. The reviews were all positive, and sales were brisk, but that didn't keep us from going for even more press. Guys In Disguise were all around you. Ora and Kim Burly did their pre-show warm-up in the actor's beer tent in full costume. Unlike most performers, drag queens don't mind being noticed in costume before a show. We would all get in drag early so we could roam the Fringe grounds for an hour before the show. Strathcona became our playground. Ora, in particular, developed a rabid taste for notoriety. She would lie down on Whyte Avenue in her beaded gown at rush hour, and the rest of us would run from car to car, sticking flyers under windshield wipers. Twiggy and I would run to the big ticket board and gloat about being sold out. We partied the entire ten days, performing and celebrating and terrorizing straight boys.

The head honcho of the Fringe nearly kicked us out of the beer tent for climbing over the barrier fence in tight miniskirts. We were the Big Talk in the Big Onion...

...and then we went back to our lives. And suddenly, the Underground seemed too dark, too closed, too rigid, too afraid of the light.

And my dragmother hated me.

And all we had was some newspaper clippings and the memory of the applause ringing in our ears... and a strange new sense of respect from some of the Underground.

And the glamor *Journal* photo shoot ended up enlarged and framed and hanging at the International Airport, believe it or not. Until 1995, it was the first image of Edmonton you saw as you arrived through international customs. To this day, if we're recognized from that photo, the girls at the counter won't charge us extra for traveling with seventy-pound beaded gowns, and awkward hatboxes filled with crowns.

Twiggy, Kim Burly, Neon, Gloria, Shanann, Ora Fice, Tallulah,
Nellie Michael
1987

Some Edmonton Queens (5)

Gloria, Cleo and Zola at Cleo's coronation, 1988

Zola, 1988.
It was the custom to dress the Mr. Flashback in girl drag
at some point in his reign.

Ora Fice 1987

DARRIN HAGEN

Heavy Is The Wig
That Wears The Crown

"I'm still big–it's the dresses that got smaller."
- Lulu LaRude

It's hard to describe the impact of a Coronation on your drag career.

The Queen you were has to be redrawn. The next year of your life has to be dedicated completely to your adoring public: the civilians that voted you in. Tthey have come to expect a certain standard of excellence–and you have to be that fabulous three nights a week for a whole year, with a new look, a new number, unflagging enthusiasm, superhuman fashion sense, and the liquor tolerance of a sailor on leave. All for free.

Let's see Princess Di do that. Mind you, she'll never be a Queen. Not with that wardrobe.

When your year was up, you passed the glory, willingly or not, to the new generation. Then you stepped as graciously as you could into the hallowed ranks of The Hall Of Dowagers. (That's drag language for has-been.) All this meant was you no longer were in control, but the Dowagers still lurked in the vicinity, waiting for the new girl to fuck things up bad enough for them to rush in and save the day.

Lulu and I were both Dowagers when Tallulah gave birth to her first daughter, my granddaughter, Lulu's great-granddaughter:

Ora Fice.

From the very beginning, Lulu and Ora didn't see eye to eye. Ora was a strange creature: devious, ambitious, desperately seeking something. Things between Lulu and I were already strained, and the pressures of matriarchy were taking a toll. Ora merely complicated things.

Ora Fice and boy Gloria 1987

DARRIN HAGEN

She Stoops To Conquer
1986-1987

"I'd like to thank the little people..."
- Ora's Acceptance Speech

After Ora was cremated, I carried her ashes around in my car for a couple of months. Not all of her ashes, 'cause she had been divided into eight or nine "bundles". Everyone at the service got a "bundle" for themselves.

I wanted to do something appropriate. But until I decided, she would just have to wait. So she stayed in the back of my car, along with some scripts, empty diet Pepsi bottles and the other stuff that collects if you don't clean your car regularly.

There were two services for Ora, each very different in nature. This matched her schizophrenic nature perfectly. She was simultaneously someone you had to tolerate, yet wanted to be around. Her career—a meteoric rise from drunken fag party boy obscurity to Diva Empress—was a two-sided-split-personality-in-your-face-blind-ambition-tiara-at-any-cost kind of time.

Drag was taking a turn away from content and towards surface glass bead glam. The Americans were having an undue influence. Yankee Empresses had big jewelry, big lashes, big hair, big egos. Ora bought the whole philosophy and became more American than Americans.

People were tools of the trade for Ora—Friends as Fodder for Fame: a means, not an end. If you could help make her more famous, more beautiful, or more stylish, she would keep you around. A lot.

Her boyfriend was a dress designer. How convenient. She had fresh gowns for every show. Her look was simple at first.

Tall, thin, manicured, neat wig pulled back into a pony tail with a huge bow that always always always matched the dress, which was tailored, elegant and simple. Gradually that transformed (in the post–Empress years) into 40 bugle beads per square inch, earrings heavier than me, and red hair glued into a massive tidal wave sweeping over one eye.

In the early years you could watch Ora soak up information like a makeup sponge. She would see what worked, and steal it. Intellectual property wasn't a term she really understood. She ran for Empress at an early age, but her style was still too wild, too unpredictable. She would perform a Latin number covered in real fruit which would fall off, banana by orange, turning to mush as she cavorted on stage. Or the Christmas show where she walked onto the stage decorated like a tree. The tinsel and twinkling lights looked great until she started dancing, then mayhem struck: glass balls shattering and popping as they gave up holding onto her dress, a heavy orange extension cord emerging from her crotch area, snaking across the stage and disappearing into the sound booth. Barbra Streisand's "Jingle Bells" will never sound the same.

Ora was the Queen of costume interruptus.

She lost her first bid to be Empress. She was conquered in battle by an older queen named Beverly Crest. Ora had to settle for second place in the palace for a year. That's when she became the mistress of court intrigue, blatantly manipulative, seductively scandalous, mysterious and mischievous. Princess Power Politics became her most important talent. She waited in the wings, watching and wanting. Everyone knew she would be the next ruler.

Then along came Yoda.

I struggle for a moment to find a delicate manner of phrasing this next information, but graceful turns of tongue momentarily elude me.

Yoda was a midget drag queen.

For someone like Ora, for whom image equaled life, the remotest possibility of losing the crown she had fought so hard for to—well—a vertically challenged person was unthinkable.

Yoda shopped in the junior petite section and did Anne Murray numbers. Her humble origins as Chastity in the Sonny & Cher performance that won me my Mz. Flashback crown had given her a new attitude. She was also becoming famous as dwarf tossing swept the bar scene.

Yoda had the advantage of a novelty vote. How many other cities could successfully hold a circus themed drag ball? There was also the outside chance that she would get elected as a joke.

But Ora had planned for too long. Something had to be done. But what? A new proclamation: "Must be taller than this line to run for Empress"? In a secret meeting, the candidate committee ruled Yoda's application invalid.

Then, all hell broke loose.

Since word had gotten out, Yoda had garnered more support than anyone had anticipated. Who could have known? Somehow the concept of a 3½-foot monarch didn't freak out the electorate. Lulu suddenly decided she would be the defender of Midget's Rights. Lulu hated Ora, and all she needed was an excuse to complicate things. This was it.

So Ora watched in horror as the ranks of Yoda's supporters swelled. People even defected to the other side once the movement started to pick up momentum. Ball weekend was approaching and the numbers were dangerously close.

Ora and Gloria 1987

The candidate committee finally relented and allowed Yoda to run. Her campaign poster had a black and white picture of her standing against a white wall in her apartment, trying to avoid comparisons of her height to any furniture in the room. However, the photographer didn't notice the electrical socket, low on the wall. It came up to Yoda's waistline.

Ora's performances began to feel a little desperate, like the stakes were getting higher. She would be the laughing stock of the ball circuit if all this glamour didn't sway people back to her camp. She had people coming from all over North America to witness her spectacular victory. She couldn't risk the sideshow.

The public was now viewing her as the enemy in the Dwarfgate scandal. Somehow it had all become her fault. Lulu fueled the furor with constant reminders of the evil irresponsible things Ora had done over the years. Ora started to panic. She of the wild wicked past saw it come seeping back to haunt her.

It was time to pull out the stops. The stunts began. Ora, in a last ditch effort, returned to her roots: insanity. She did the craziest things anyone had seen. She went into a pre-vote binge-party-week. New rumors started: Ora had been spotted on roller-skates being pulled by a station wagon down Fourth Street in a tutu in broad daylight; she rolled her mother's car and walked away from the wreck, laughing, and went back into the bar.

And the big finish: Police were called to the Palisades downtown to arrest a transvestite climbing the outside of the building balcony by balcony—in full glamour drag. Dorky was hosting the Barbie Sacrifice party, and Ora, who lived in the same highrise, decided on a new route to Dorky's forteenth-floor apartment.

Opinion began to swing back. She was still the final word inglamour, but if it was a circus people wanted, she was only too willing to comply.

And somehow—it worked.

She won by a landslide and was crowned Empress XII.

Maybe it was just people coming back to their senses, or maybe something in her reckless overdressed passion struck a chord in the rest of us. To see someone desire something so badly that she would risk life and lash to climb a downtown high-rise was an inspiring sight.

Her year as Empress was the zenith of the glamour years. She set a new standard for beaucoup de gownage. She traveled extensively, wooing and wowing the circuit.

She had balls.

I kept all of this in mind as I drove around looking for a place to scatter the ashes. I had actually been spreading her here and there, as I saw locations that seemed significant.

Whyte Avenue and Fifth Street where she had stopped traffic in full drag in all four directions. The old Flashback alley where we had stumbled into cabs in broad daylight with beards growing through our makeup. Off a balcony at the Palisades, of course. A Greek restaurant where she had used her press-on nails to spear food off people's plates as she walked through.

Two final images . . .

At one of Ora's memorials, we went outside afterwards for a smoke. There in the parking lot was a car with the trunk open. Seven queens clustered around, and for a moment I couldn't figure out that they were doing. Then I saw a flash of glitter, and realized they were divvying up Ora's drag. The trunk was overflowing with dresses, crowns, jewels, capes. All up for sale. Cheap. Everything must go.

Like seven grotesque vultures tearing at a beaded carcass. Devouring what she was. Ora was what she wore. What she was disappeared into separate bags and was deposited in separate trunks in separate cars that drove away in the rain.

The second memorial, I held her in my hands. Ashes are kind of like gravel. We each got a white balloon, and after speaking we let the balloons go.

Brilliant sunlight.

The white balloons floating higher and higher and further and further until they disappeared in a blur of tears, the fog of memory, like some sad, languid, beautiful dream.

Some stars burn so brightly they consume themselves.

Cleo 1988

All That Glitters...
1988

"Women and children first!"
- Sister Neon

Bianca Bang-Bang, Dorky and I sat eating lunch downtown one day, when we saw a sight that made us all stop chewing our baguettes.

"Girl, look at that," chortled Bianca.

Even by our standards, the person we were watching crossed a few gender lines. It was the Michael Jackson "Thriller" jacket that caught our attention first, the mohawk second. But when we heard this young black man's voice as he ordered the soup of the day, all three of us snorted into our soup.

He sounded even more like Michael Jackson than he looked: whispery and girly, like a black Marilyn Monroe. He caught us staring at him, so we looked away quickly, not wanting to appear too rude.

"Ten bucks says we see *her* at the club by Saturday," I said sarcastically.

Saturday arrived. And so did she.

Within a couple of months, she had stolen everyone's heart. Within a year, she was

Cleo.

There's a special place in the world for people who remain eternally young, refusing all attempts at growing up. Regardless of how old she actually was, she inspired protection and motherly instincts in all of us. What at first seemed outrageously queeny gradually became endearing, then addictively funny. Her small stature and big mouth meant it was only a matter of time before we talked her into crossing the line.

For Cleo, that line was a place where you celebrated with laughter, where beauty was something you didn't take too seriously, unless it could get you free cocktails. She quickly learned the power of youth combined with beauty, then sabotaged it before it could be pinned on her as a character trait. She would work for weeks on a performance, then trash the entire thing on-stage by letting her wig fly off.

The audience approved.

Cleo started out as part of a team. Much like I had found Lulu in those crucial formative years, she found her soul mate: Gracie Spoon.

The two of them, both young, black, proud and insane, were inseparable. Together they began the rise through the ranks of influence. But when they created comedy, the world lay laughing at their feet and begged to be put out of its misery.

Their weapon: The Lipps Sisters.

The two of them had been working on a serious drag duet for ages: "I Know Him So Well" by Whitney and Cissy Houston. For two black girls, a love duet sung by the Divas-to-end-all-Divas was a dream come true. But, as usual, Cleo started getting cold feet before the show. She was never totally at ease with the ease of her beauty.

Minutes before showtime, Cleo changed her mind. She disappeared into the back without a word, and when she re-appeared, she had become a clown.

Gone was the immaculate Supremes hair: she had teased it

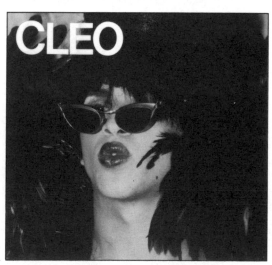

impossibly high and decorated it with cocktail umbrellas. Gone was the stunning evening gown: she had replaced it with a Value Village Mumu from the drag pit.

And gone was the perfect makeup she had spent hours fussing over: Cleo had repainted her lips so that they took over her face.

Her lips took over her face...

Cleo, 1988ish

Clown with no conscience.

When Gracie spotted her, she shrieked.

The show was only minutes away. It was too late to do anything but follow suit.

Gracie swallowed her pride and conformed.

When The Lipps Sisters hit the stage, camp met crazy and a Drag Classic was born. The Lipps Sisters were an overnight sensation, leaving trails of polyester-lined hilarity wherever they performed. Cleo and Gracie became the new toast of the Big Onion.

It was only a matter of time before they began to hunger for the crown.

Much like Lulu and I, Gracie and Cleo lived together, performed and partied together, laughed and cried together. Also like Lulu and I, Gracie wanted to be Empress and Cleo coveted the Mz. Flashback crown.

They took over the scene within months.

That's when envy reared its ugly green head.

Cleo's love of life, laughter and the pursuit of fabulous hair didn't exactly mesh with Gracie's ambitions. She gradually saw the spotlight favoring Cleo, the way attention is showered on a favorite child. Bit by bit, friendship evaporated into a good-natured rivalry, then collided head-on with out-and-out jealousy. Gracie was definitely the boss, but her little sister was hungrily lapping up all the praise and adoration that the mob had to offer.

By this time, both had been adopted into the Family: Gracie as my foster daughter, and Cleo as Tallulah's's foster daughter. There was room for everyone, or so we thought.

When Ora stepped down as Empress, Gracie was the favored candidate to win. While she waited in the wings for the new ruler to be announced, Cleo was already the new Mz. Flashback. And as always, the audience breathlessly awaited the Flashback entrance.

We had been working for weeks on the performance. Cleo would be Christine in "Phantom", hauled into the Ballroom by slaves pulling a huge gondola on wheels. She would glide up to the dais, dismount and wow the crowd with her beauty and poise.

Or, at least, that was the plan.

The gondola was a work of art. Seven feet high, with a curved, Viking-like front. Constructed by someone who had a way with power tools, it glided effortlessly in all the test runs, even with a queen on board. The whole affair was sprayed with a clear adhesive, and then covered in red glitter. It caught the light magically, like a glitzy Loch Ness Monster. I could picture the reaction as it floated through the ballroom.

There was only one problem: the glue wouldn't dry.

That was fine, we thought, as there was still a week until the ball.

A week later, the glue still hadn't dried. You couldn't touch the gondola without your hand coming away covered in red glitter. "Don't touch the gondola!" Cleo would scream at anyone that was admiring it. And we still had to figure out how to get it to the hotel for the Ball, let alone how to drag it up to the dais without getting glittered to death.

So we assigned the task of transporting it to two butch staff members, while we packed up our costumes and headed to the Ball. We were behind schedule, but that was par for the course; Drag Time meant we were probably right on time.

As we entered the Ballroom, we realized that for the first time in history the Ball had actually started on time. Ora, trying to prove some point about her organizational skills, had insisted that the time posted was the actual time it would start. This threw the entire evening into a panic. As we stood there with Cleo, scanning the Ballroom for our reserved Flashback table, we heard:

"Ladies and gentlemen, the Reigning Mz. Flashback, Cleo!"

Cleo's campaign poster 1988

We looked at each other in disbelief as the "Phantom" music started. We had just entered the room! We were nowhere near ready. Neon screamed, "Cut the music!" and headed to the emcee to plead for more time, as we frantically searched the badly lit backstage for our costumes, swearing, pushing queens out of our way as we emptied bags onto the floor.

Of course, we had forgotten all the robes for the slaves. In fact, the only ones who had remembered their costumes were Cleo and her Mr. Flashback, Zola.

"Here, wear this", shouted Neon as she threw whatever she could find at all the backup. We would just have to make do. We draped fabric around us, trying to make it look like a style choice. We were ready to completely make up the whole entrance.

But the gondola finally arrived as we stood in the wings, ready to go on.

We were saved! We lifted Cleo into the gondola. Immediately, her $500 gown received a shock of red glitter up the backside. "Don't touch the gondola!" she screamed, frantically trying to brush it off. The wet glue just smeared, spreading the glitter to her hands.

We stood, stoic, serious, and waited for the music to start. Zola took his place on the ramp, wearing his Phantom mask. The first organ chords flew through the air.

We took a deep breath and began pulling the gondola into the Ballroom. The crowd cheered, recognizing the music immediately, as they always did.

The walk leading up to the dais was about forty feet long, and covered in red carpet for that pseudo-regal feel. *This will be fabulous,* I thought, picturing how we must look as we floated into view.

Then the gondola stopped short, with a mighty jerk that almost threw Cleo onto the floor.

The red carpet had bunched up under the wheels and frozen it in place.

The slaves tugged, trying to get past the sticking point. They succeeded, almost knocking Cleo over again in the process. Then five feet later, it happened again. This time, however, the carpet was so piled, the slaves couldn't budge it. They looked up at Cleo, wondering what to do next. One of them went to grab the sides to push. "DON'T TOUCH THE GONDOLA!" screamed Cleo.

Finally, exasperated past the point of politeness, Cleo rolled her eyes. "FUCK IT!" she exclaimed, loud enough that it was audible over the blaring Lloyd-Weber. She hoisted up the voluminous skirts of her $500 gown and climbed out of the gondola, marched up to the dais and finished her number.

The crowd clapped politely, but we all knew the Entrance had been ruined.

Flashback won the Best Entrance award that night, but it was obviously out of sheer pity. The gondola ended up in the dumpster outside Flashback the next day.

A week later, before the garbage truck picked up the refuse, I went and touched the gondola.

The glue had finally dried.

Gracie became the new Empress, then started her own drag family.

Lulu and I immediately banished her for her betrayal.

Cry Me A River

1990

Tallulah's reign ended triumphantly, and gave way to the sophistication of Twiggy. Twiggy passed the crown to **Kim Burly**, my second daughter. The thirteenth Mz. Flashback was Cleo, spawn of Tallulah and Ora's foster sister, who bequeathed the title to **Gretchen Wilder**, Ora's insane daughter.

The last year of the Dynasty was 1990. **Christine**, a very convincing sex change, beat all the drag competition and became the first transgender crowned in the Big Onion. She didn't last the year, however. Partway through the year, she resigned and gave the crown to Leah Weigh. Leah decided she would rather be Empress, however, and bequeathed the title to Ginger Snapped, who move to Florida to become a big drag star. She left the crown in the care of **Mandy Kamp**, Ora's Princess and eldest daughter.

Mandy was the last Mz. Flashback.

She never stepped down. There was no Flashback by the time the year was up.

The glass brick wall was dismantled and moved out in the middle of the night. Pieces of it, and the rest of the club, moved to garages and basements all over the city.

When Flashback closed its doors, an era of Edmonton's Underground history was officially over. The scene still exists, but can no longer boast the shining jewel of the Prairies. The evil landlords evicted the Family so they could turn the warehouse into condos.

By the time it happened, Lulu had been gone a couple of years, which was just as well. She didn't have to see what happened. She didn't have to watch our lives get hauled to the dumpster, or see the rage as the staff, evicted from their Home, kicked in walls and broke windows.

She had gone to Toronto to do a pro show. She never came back.

And the Family, with no Matriarch and no Home, drifted around the world and lost contact. With no escape from reality, we faced the light and started our new lives.

Our time together in the Big Onion ended pretty silently for two people as loud as we were. We drifted like ice floes for a time, bumping off each other, sometimes connecting, often missing. Egos had been bruised, feelings hurt, things said...

The Club that ate Edmonton slipped away and sank under the water; the Titanic of fag bars. We had all assumed she was unsinkable, that she would float forever, taking us to warmer places, but taking us.

Our lives, like lifeboats left after a disaster, seemed awfully small for a while. And lonely.

And the body count hadn't even started yet.

The very last Mr. & Mz. Flashback party, May 23, 1989.
This was also the last time we were all together while everyone was still alive.
Back row: Nellie Michael, Zola, Dorky, Twiggy, Tallulah, Gloria
Centre row: Bianca Bang-Bang, Cleo, Neon, Mr. K.
Front row: Trash, Millie, Gretchen

The Truth About Fried Eggs

"'Cause the truth about fried eggs, see,
Is you can call it anything you want...
But everybody's got one.
Some people wear them on the inside,
and some wear them on the outside."
- Bette Midler, "Live At Last"

People sometimes ask how an otherwise reasonable young man could turn his back on everything and dive Underground. What makes a person pull out of the world of Men and Women and strike out on his own, reinventing Gender like it was something to be shed at the earliest possible convenience, laughing in the faces of the people most baffled by it, throwing their pain and confusion into full view where it was most visible?

The truth is, for most of these men, that they were never whole until they made peace with the very part of themselves that society damned. They all looked in the mirror early in life and tried to figure out why they seemed so unusual. What did people see that made them so dangerous, the target of abuse and mockery? When they finally looked into the looking glass and saw her, the woman they had been avoiding all their lives, the one inside, every male instinct of protection sprung into action. Suddenly they had someone to protect. Suddenly they all became valuable. To themselves.

Suddenly someone mattered.

There isn't a more public therapy on the market. There are no how-to books. You learn the art from the artists themselves. Your personal growth happens on stage and in the public eye and in glamour photo shoots.

Under the ostrich-feather wing of your sister-mother-goddess figure, the real world disappears. All the garbage you're fed about being a man is revealed for what it is: control.

Because if you don't control men, there is the chance that they may figure it out. They may see through the dogma-infested fear-mongering paranoia that is life in the twentieth century and realize: it's all a lie.

The man they want you to be doesn't exist. He has to be created. By Men.

Men are controlled by Men's controls. Defending their power, they become controlled by it. And the men they can't control are exiled.

Out of sight, out of mind.

But some men refuse to stay out of sight. Crossing the line of control takes the very elements that terrify men and dresses them up and shoves them straight back in their crotches.

Every time a red-blooded hetero boy is attracted, even for a split second, to that strange Amazon on the dance floor, what is he responding to? Femaleness? Hardly. More like the trappings. His blood stirs in response to the stuff we put on: the big tits, the impossible curves, the come-fuck-me attitude, the unnatural padding, the torturous shoes...

He responds to all the stuff women have spent decades discarding in their quest for equal footing.

He responds to a woman created completely by another man, using all the repressive techniques men have wished upon women to turn them into fantasy objects, most of which were invented by men.

Who's got the power now, baby?

The men that crossed the line reached a new stage of evolution–whether they knew it or not. By casting off the man they became more human.

Drag says a lot more about men than it does about women. That's why it hurts so much when some women say drag is misogynistic. On the contrary; it's the most feminist thing a man can do.

There's nothing like walking in someone else's shoes for discovering how much they hurt.

Some Edmonton Queens (6)

Twiggy, Mandy and Kim Burly in Guys in Disguise, 1991

Ginger Snot, Lindee, Mrs. K (The Razzberries) and Gloria
Beverly Crest's ball at the Holiday Inn, 1987

If the shoes hurt, wear 'em. Gloria, 1989

Gloria the mermaid,
afloat in front of Edmonton City Hall

DARRIN HAGEN

A Fish Out Of Water
August 1994
Downtown Edmonton

"Let's just say only a few kids cried."
- Christopher Peterson
(about performing at Family Day)

Festival City. Or, at least, that's what *we* call it. Some misguided civic politician decided, at some point, to nickname The Big Onion "The City Of Champions".

Then Gretzky was traded to L.A. and the local team stopped winning.

Someone should have told that politician not to brag. Trophies mean little once they've moved on. But the mentality of the men who run this province has always been dubious, to say the least. They decided that "champions" were what this city was most famous for, and erected a large sign on the outskirts proudly proclaiming that fact.

The trophy never came home again.

Years ago, Lulu and I had decided that what they probably meant was "City Of Champignons", but not wanting to spark up a heated bilingual debate, we let it go.

What The Big Onion is truly remarkable for is its dynamic summer festival season. Starting in June, the locals could consecutively view world class jazz, visual arts, folk music, theater, even street performers.

I watched Sir Winston Churchill Square that summer as it throbbed with families. The true heart of downtown, it was the home of many celebrations. City Hall presided over the proceedings with a stately air. Next to it stood that clock tower where my ill-fated New Year's Eve go-go experience had happened. But it would be different, this time.

For one thing, it wasn't minus forty degrees outside.

Actually, it was blistering hot. Big Onion summers are a thing to behold: hour after endless hour of sunlight so bright it hurt. Especially now, at noon, when shadows shrunk to nothing and there was no escape from the heat.

Being in drag in heat like that presents as many problems as cranking in mid-winter. Makeup melts at thirty degrees.

It was thirty-five above[3], and I was once again beginning to question my judgment. As always, the concept had sounded good on paper.

Ever since that first Fringe parade, my mermaid costume had become a camera magnet. Pull the tail on, and watch the fun begin. I had been photographed in it enough times that it had become a very recognizable image. And with the release of Disney's "The Little Mermaid", it seemed like an even better idea to dig the old fish tail out of the mothballs and give it a run. My mermaid tail was exactly the same shade of aquamarine as Disney's, even though mine had been constructed three years earlier. It had gotten me onto the front page of the *Journal* two summers in a row.

It was not without its problems, however. Once the tail was on, movement was next to impossible, unless you were a champion hopper. It consisted of a foam tail that your feet slipped into, then a spandex tube that pulled up like one leg of a giant pair of pantyhose. A matching bikini top with built-in foamies pulled on over the head like a t-shirt, placed over the nipples. It was notorious for slipping and revealing at crucially public times.

It was also an outfit in which a tuck was of paramount importance. Spandex is the single most merciless fabric when it comes to what you're trying to hide underneath it. The practicalities of this complex ritual is one I've been steering to avoid, but it is unique to the art form, and deserves at least a brief passage of explanation.

A "tuck" is the process of removing penile evidence in the crotch area, usually only important in tight, revealing outfits. It is generally performed with a dance belt, but a good queen should be able to tuck with a roll of duct tape and a rubber band.

Lulu used to refer to the process as being remarkably similar to Glad sandwich bags: flip, flop, fold the top. Let's just say you're sitting on your own testicles all night.

---

[3] Celsius: about 95 Fahrenheit

And the only thing in the world that hurts more than being in tuck is taking it out at the end of the night.

But I digress.

This was the plan:

Meet the Street Performer staff boy at the info booth, with a ladder. My shift starts at noon. I arrive in a long coat, to hide the fact that I'm wearing only a tiny aquamarine Speedo as a foundation garment. (Mother used to say: "What if you're in a car accident in drag and your underwear isn't colour-coordinated?") Ladder-boy and I rendezvous at the information booth. He looks at me oddly. I remember that I have a full face of makeup and a long red wig on. But I'm also in bare feet, because you can't have footwear with a mermaid tail. My tail is in a green garbage bag by my side. He leans the ladder against the aluminum booth and I scamper up to the roof, garbage bag in tow.

As soon as I'm on the roof, I see the ladder pulling away. Some high-wire jugglers need it for their show, and it'll be back at the end of my shift: two o'clock. I sit, trying to figure out how to deal with delicately dressing in full sunlight on a hot tin roof in a park filled with packs of daycare field trips, the main audience at that early hour. I decide that if I just do it efficiently and quickly, it won't attract much attention.

With my back to the park and my legs dangling over the edge of the info booth, I slip my feet into the foam tail and pull up the aquamarine spandex tube. In order to get it all the way on, however, I have to do the tail-in-the-air routine, flipping it around as I stretch the fabric up. Finally it's ready. I pull on the bra-piece, spin it around until the foam covers my nipples, and voila! I'm ready. Thank God I had the good sense to tuck in the changeroom. But just in case I pop my tuck, I at least had the resource to drag along some large pieces of purple and pink chiffon, long enough to drape over my mid-section and drape to the ground, flowing in the slight breeze.

I grab my harp, and face the square.

Five minutes later, I'm already not having fun. The July sun rains down like lava, melting everything in its path. The concept of a fish on a hot tin roof that just kept getting hotter hadn't occurred to me. I have to keep shifting positions to keep from burning, and with my legs locked together in the spandex tube, there are only so many comfortable poses. I switch every time the heat becomes unbearable, repositioning the chiffon strategically, holding the harp at different angles.

My high vantage point provides me with a unique view of the park. The lunch rush is in full swing, with suits and ties and power dresses and bag lunches in view everywhere. Many people are being tormented by clowns or musicians or sundry characters. The fun thing about the street performer's life is tormenting the civilians, an echo of my former freedom Underground. The ones in disguise always have an advantage. Street performing has an edge of the dangerous built into the job.

The rest of the inhabitants are children, hundreds of them. The paltry few daycare supervisors run around like dogs, herding the kids into barely manageable circles. Their attention is diverted easily, and they move rapidly from tightrope to balloon art to sword swallowing. I am grateful for this, as my act is little more than a visual punchline. I sit, posed, on the roof.

Most of the kids can't even see that high. I'm way out of their field of vision. But I do have a couple of interactions with some children. One thing you learn quickly about kids is that they're never afraid to ask the questions the adults will only wonder silently about. A little boy comes running up, thinking I am Ariel of Disney fame.

"Look, Mommy! The mermaid!" The words are barely out of his mouth when he stops himself. His mouth drops open with disbelief. "That's a guy!"

His mother is confused; she has no framework for dealing with this. She drags him away, both of them looking back suspiciously.

A *Journal* photographer approaches. Lulu trained me to smell a photo opportunity at seventy paces. I launch into the repertoire: harp in the air, then tail up, arch wiggle wiggle, chiffon floating in the breeze, the wind beneath my wig. I am the siren, luring unsuspecting sailor boys starved for a different kind of fish, my song of seduction dragging them to their watery graves, their souls forfeited in a deadly game with only one outcome. As the reporter clicks madly, and I make love to the camera, I hear a decidedly youthful voice. It carries a note of childhood skepticism, and its sense of logic has conviction.

"Real mermaids can't get on roofs."

I look down at a small Oriental boy. He watches me closely,

ice cream cone in hand. "How come you're not in the water?" he asks, gesturing to the City Hall reflecting pool.

"Are you kidding? In this outfit, I'd drown. Do you know how much foam I'm wearing?" Some grownups laugh, but my humour is lost on the boy.

"You're a boy. Mermaids can't be boys. You're not a mermaid." He stands and says this calmly, but definitively.

I suddenly realize that in all my hours and hours of routines and comebacks and insults for controlling hostile situations, there is absolutely nothing in my arsenal for dealing with kids. I could probably deal with a drunk bunch of horny sailors better than I could hold my own with this boy's determined questions. He continues.

"I just saw your boy-tit!" he giggles. "You're a boy. You can't dress like a mermaid."

Suddenly a gaggle of daycare four year olds surround him. A lone woman watches the whole pack, barely maintaining control. Two little girls start with more probing questions.

"How did you get up there with no legs?"

"How come you're out of the water and you're not dead?"

"Why are you dressed like a girl? Boys don't wear makeup."

"You're not a mermaid. You are a man!"

The little boy picked up the chant. Then all the kids. *You are a ma-an, you are a ma-an ,...*if I just ignore them they'll stop...*you are a ma-an, you are a ma-an, you are a ma-an, you are a ma-an, you are a ma-an, you are a ma-an, you are a ma-an, you are a ma-an, you are a ma-an, you are a ma-an...*this can't go on much longer...*you are a ma-an, you are a ma-n, you are a ma-an, you are a ma-an, you are a ma-an, you are a ma-an...*why doesn't that stupid bitch teacher get them away from me...*you are a ma-an, you are a ma-an, you are a ma-an, you are a ma-an, you are a ma-an, you are a ma-an, you are a ma-an, you are a ma-an, you are a ma-an, you are a ma-an, you are a ma-an...*

For the next hour, every time they were within view, they would pick up the chant again.

I could hear them as they moved around the square. I lay there, eyes gazing up at the sun. Participation in the surroundings seemed pointless. I ignored everything, said nothing, just flapped my tail sadly if anyone talked to me.

Even at that tender age, the lines in the sandbox are so clearly drawn that those kids refused to allow me to cross over. They attacked it because they were already afraid of challenges to the Divided: the boy-girl world. They were already afraid of someone who refused to be one. Or the other.

I had forgotten that the price of being on land is your voice.

Or at least, it is for mermaids.

1994: a week or two after The Mermaid Incident

DARRIN HAGEN

I'll Be Seeing You...
1990-1997

...**This** all feels like a lifetime away...
All I have to do is remember.
Like I could ever forget.
What sounds like generations was a few years.
Each of us got the same prize, although the methods differ.
We arrived in Edmonton with no family. So we built one.
The only roots we knew were some two-bit hairdresser's mistake, yet we took root and flourished.

All of these men had one thing in common. They were willing to put themselves on hold, sometimes for up to a decade or more, while their own body and soul became a means of expression. Their own personality and maleness stepped gracefully aside to give the Inner Woman free reign.

It was life of Pumps and Circumstance. Rather than hide their pain, they strapped it on and accessorized it. Wear your shame and make it look better than God ever intended.

They became living, walking, breathing, screaming, chain-smoking Art. A live canvas ready to be tweezed, shaved, waxed, plucked, painted, glued, beaded, teased, sprayed, and ultimately displayed.

Then, like all art, viewed, perused, mocked, scorned, criticized, adored, ignored. In trying to set themselves apart, they become part of the drag/fag landscape glitzy scenery that you always see but rarely acknowledge.

Even Underground, there are those who say that drag is about covering up what you really are.

On the contrary; nothing could be more revealing. Drag showed us who we were.

Yet I know surprisingly little about the previous lives of these creatures. Much of that has vanished with them, as if they didn't really exist until they disappeared Underground. Their first act as adults was to reinvent themselves; the name they grew up with was shed immediately, and in its place a new human was born, free of the shackles and fear that characterized their early years.

I was surprised as I wrote this to realize that I knew absolutely nothing about how Lulu ended up in Edmonton. A few phone calls later, and I realized that only Lulu has that story. There was much about our lives that we shared; there were volumes more that we didn't. I know that she was an army brat, and lived in Germany, Nova Scotia and Rimbey, but not much more.

I know that Tallulah came out to her mother while she took a bath. Tallulah sat on the toilet seat and told her naked mother, "I'm gay." Her mother replied, "Don't tell your father." But not much more.

I know that Ora was predeceased by her brother, while her insane alcoholic father languished in mental home, dying soon after, and then her mother, whom I had met at the Drag Races, passed away after a long battle with heart disease. I also learned a couple of days ago that Ora had been gang-raped by her brother and his friends. But not much more.

We went Underground to hide from ourselves. Instead, we discovered ourselves.

In every world, there are two universes: the one you see, and the one you refuse to see.

A decade has now passed since Guys In Disguise first appeared on the Surface. At the time, it seemed no more than a chance to do a show and make some cash doing what we loved doing. It took me years to realize that it was a crucial period in all of our development; a tiny act of defiance that changed every one of us forever.

You don't change the world by doing what it tells you to do.

The world has gone through some big changes. So much has happened in that decade.

Tallulah died in 1993. It had been two years since we had spoken. Like most mothers and daughters, we were never great about keeping in touch. Our last visit was chock full of the all-night marathon talks for which she was so famous. She climbed on her Italian soapbox a few times, telling me off, telling off the world but I was the only one there. It didn't matter as long as someone could hear.

She told me about getting full vision for the first time in her life, in her twenties. She got goose bumps describing the shade of blue of the surgeon's uniform as he peeled the bandages from her eyes.

It was the first color other than black that she had seen in years.

I had heard the story before, but I cried anyway.

Tallulah's last hurrah: stepping down as Imperial Crown Princess XX in Vancouver, 1992, she wrote a last message to everyone in her life.

Then she asked why I was the only one who didn't cry when she told me she was going to die.

I still don't have an answer for that one.

Her last reign was as Imperial Princess to Moira in Vancouver. In her step-down message, she took her last brutally honest jab at everyone in her life. To her daughter Ora, a haunting riddle: *It's too bad you never reached out for the help you obviously needed.*

She died angry. The disease was just one more strike, and she was tired of this game. Her old-world mother, speaking no English

Tallulah /Luano, early 1990s

but understanding all, was by her bedside.

Excretia died in Toronto. She just disappeared from our lives. She spent her last days in the care of her mother. The image of an ordinary Maritime woman looking after the skinhead drag queen who had terrorized The Big Onion so many years ago is a striking one.

Death is the mighty equalizer.

Iona and Lulu, late 1980s
Iona died April 14, 1996

Iona's poetry was published in the first edition of an award winning play. The award came after she, too, had returned to the Okanagan, to die with her family present.

At some point, the Family we had created stopped being enough. Dragmothers faded in the picture as real mothers reentered the drama to care for their boys.

Priorities change when your children are threatened. Ironically, the very thing that distanced these boys from their families drew them back together for one final time. Life is to be valued, regardless of how it is lived. Time became precious as these mothers struggled to match the son they knew with the film noir movie star photos on the wall and the tiaras in the trophy case; a sudden desperate need to understand while it mattered, while it could still make a difference.

The value of life skyrocketed.

In a cruel twist of fate, Ora became an orphan again when Tallulah went to that Spotlight in the Sky. Ora's real mother had died years earlier, but not before her brother and father passed on. Ora stood alone.

She died two springs ago. I got the message on my answering machine. She had been dead a few days when they found her on her living room floor. All her furniture was piled up against the door to the apartment.

Who knows what she was trying to keep out.

Two long-lost aunts emerged from the woodwork to fight over the insurance money. Her gowns were sold in the parking lot at the funeral home to pay for the service. We were the only real family there.

Millie left this world in 1996, twenty years after she began the system that would dominate our lives for so many years. The partying finally did her in. She was found in her room on skid row. Her body disappeared for a while before the funeral, in an eerie Marilyn Monroe-type mystery, but was recovered just in time.

Millie lay in an unmarked grave for over a year, until Empress XXI Natasha raised money through a drag show for a tombstone[4]. Two decades after she first laid the groundwork for an alternative universe, the system lives on. And on.

Trash and his sculpture keeping watch, early 1990s

I caught up with Trash in Vancouver. Actually, a news camera crew found her. For years, massive stone art was appearing around the sea wall overlooking English Bay. No one could explain these freestanding feats of balance; rumours abounded as to who was building them and what they meant.

[4] Shortly after that, Natasha was stripped of her title for all time. "Conduct unbecoming" was the official reason.

Finally, a work in progress was captured on film: there was Trash, more mature but still wiry and muscular, hoisting rocks and driftwood twice his own weight and freebalancing them repeatedly until they stayed in place through sheer willpower. As always, Trash rearranged landscape until it suited his mood. The giant sculptures, constructed out of the refuse of the sea, stood silhouetted against the sunset, silently keeping watch over the spot in the bay where his brother's ashes were scattered.

As usual, Trash took no credit until forced to. Art for him was like breathing: it just happened while you lived.

Every life is a work of art; every piece of art changes the world.

Atlantic Lulu
Peggy's Cove, 1995

DARRIN HAGEN

Lulu lives in Halifax. God help the east coast. I hear she's taken the town by storm. No surprise. Lulu cornered the market on charisma years ago. She presides over the Atlantic like a Zen Mother, spawning Holes with abandon, creating rich histories, family ties that, for a moment, bind together the Outcast Elite; the Lucky ones that get to see it all. Under her great wings the real world disappears.

Tina, Mandy, Mrs. K. and Cleo reside in Vancouver. Kim Burly finally moved to Calgary, where Lindee Star also lives. Bianca Bang-Bang moved to Texas, then Kentucky. Twiggy, Neon and Gretchen still terrorize Edmonton, only now they're the Old Guard.

It's all a matter of perspective.

Iona, Ginger Snot, Prickles, Lori St. John, Zola, Reena, and Joeboy are all dead now.

Most moved away to die. It's the ones left behind that hurt.

I stood on the High Level Bridge and opened the last of Ora's ashes. She scattered in the wind, falling into the river, disappearing into the murky flow. The water was brown, not blue. It's the same river, but older. It carries more within itself.

My Girls.

They knew how to live. Then they learned how to die.

Robbed of years of majesty, decades of potential.

Most of them didn't reach thirty.

It's easy to forget that all of these people are men. We were all "she"s back then. I still call them that. Respect for the art they created, the art they embodied.

The drag they wore was no different than the drag every human dons every day of his/her life, every time they present anything other than what they actually are. Drag may be a disguise, but it's also an illumination. It clearly tells people how you want to be perceived.

That being said, even if I never wear another dress as long as I live, I remain, and will always be, a Queen.

We all were. Are.

So here's to Men like us.

We came from farms and cities and fishing villages and oil rig towns and dysfunctional families and well-adjusted families and ministers' families. We are your hairdressers, your bank tellers, your mailmen, your teachers, your brothers, your sons, that hot guy that moved in next door.

We lived among you.

We lived with abandon.

We lived here, in spite of the rules, in spite of ourselves.

We lived fast and hard and dangerous lives, and most of you never noticed.

We lived.

All we had in common was an age old awareness that somehow we were different at the very core.

This isn't about not being good at hockey.

It's about knowing from the word go that in a world of men and women, you are neither.

And both.

Their names are all now legend Underground. The land they ruled over churns on and on without them. You can't stop time. Crowns get passed around like rhinestone cookie cutters. Prizes for being the most... whatever it is at the moment.

But here on earth, there are just big empty spaces where they used to be.

Every time I hear one of their old drag numbers, a snapshot pops into view–sculpted hair, lips quivering, arms stretched out at the standup mike, the brilliant spotlight cascading down, then breaking like a million mirrors, refracted by jewels into shattering beams until we were blinded, their eyes gazing upward, sparkling with life and emotion and passion for their separateness, their existence, that moment... like their whole life culminated on that stage in that moment, that shining, perfect moment...

The Applause.

The Lucky Ones.

Everyone should feel that before they die.

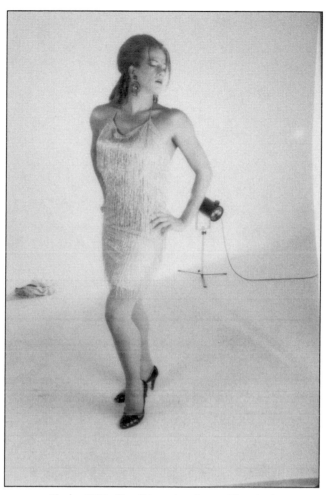

Gloria, 1996, *The Edmonton Queen* (the play)

"...and did I ever tell you
that when I was little
I would stand under a street lamp
and pretend
that I
was a beam
of light?"

–Stephen Dyson
a.k.a. Iona Box

DARRIN HAGEN

Gloria, Lulu and Justine, Gay Pride Parade, Toronto 1990ish

The Queen's English
(a lip glossary)

amateur night: Hallowe'en.
anchor: the best number in a show. Usually the last, and usually the reigning queen.
ball: a yearly gathering of queens, bidding the previous dynasty farewell, and crowning the new Monarchs.
barbies: blond female heterosexuals.
Barry-T's wannabees: straight people who go to fag bars because they're more fun and the music is better.
the Big Onion: Edmonton, Alberta
the big shave: face, chest, armpits and stomach. (Never legs, if you can help it. That's what multiple layers of pantyhose are for.)
black bathing suit: a mythic piece of clothing that Lulu searched for every time she did drag for four years. Its actual existence has never been verified, but according to her, it formed the foundation for everything she had ever planned on wearing.
boing-boing-turn-around: how Barbies dance.
"borrowing": wearing something without asking the permission of the queen it belongs to.
breast: anything used to stuff a bra. Possibilities include

foamies, nylons filled with rice or popcorn (unpopped), balloons, water balloons, toilet paper or socks (that way, you know where they are when you get out of drag).

breeders: heterosexuals.

chomp: an expression to show appreciation for a studly male specimen.

the Circuit: the tour of North America's Ball schedule.

cocksucker red: the perfect shade of lipstick.

come-fuck-me pumps: an essential wardrobe item.

cookie cutter: crown.

costume interruptus: something falling off as you perform.

Cowtown: Calgary, Alberta.

crank: to do drag.

derelicts: young, cute, "straight" boys that management bribes with liquor to pretty up the place on the promise that they will eventually put out.

dowager: a queen who has stepped down. (Also referred to as "Dogwagger".)

drag hag: a straight girl who prefers the company of queens.

drag pit: the dressing room/ costume storage.

drag time: one or two hours later than the actual time posted.

eating dead babies: getting caught with lipstick on your teeth.

elected boy titles: the man on your arm while you have a crown. Sometimes an equal partner, sometimes a glorified escort.

Empress: a title given to the queen who wins the most votes at the Ball. She then represents the city's drag community for a year.

Empress damage: the ego alteration that occurs after you've possessed a crown. *see also: glitzworm.*

Gloria and Trash 1989
In front of "the deadbeat list"
at the main bar at Flashback

fag hag: a straight girl who wants to sleep with fags.

fish: a derogatory term for female.

Flashback: a private gay bar, where drag queens ruled.

The Foxy Lady: a bar next door to Flashback. The name

says it all. On average, three ambulances a week would arrive to deal with the wounded.

fruit fly: a straight chick who prefers partying with fags.

genderfuck drag: part of the punk movement. Androgyny with a touch of S&M thrown in.

the Girls: whoever you were out with in drag.

the glitzworm: the bug. Legend claimed that the glitzworm lived in the drag pit, disguised with pieces of discarded sequins, feathers, or tinsel. While you were sitting at the head mirror, the glitzworm would sneak up to you (invisible because of its camouflage) and insert a long, hollow tongue in your ear and inject your brain with a poison that made you think you were always on-stage and always beautiful. There is no known antidote. *see also: Empress damage.*

gorillapause: hairy hands.

great moments in spork: an embarrassing drag moment caught on film or video (i.e.. popping a tuck on stage, passing out in drag, giving head in the handicapped stall in the ladies' can, etc.)

green: the spotlight colour you shine on queens you hate.

harem: the group of girls, ex-girlfriends and wives of straight disc jockeys.

the hassle team: a group of queens that follow the beat cops through the club being annoying.

Some Edmonton Queens (7)

Neon and Twiggy

Trash

high drag: beaded gowns, tiaras and piled hair.

the Hill: where teenage hustler boys work. Particularly busy just after last call.

husbands: the police.

Jasper Avenue: the Big Onion's main street.

Klondike Days: a Big Onion event (for straight people) at which the whole city is forced to wear outfits even a queen would eschew (*Editor's note: Bless you!*).

kool-aid lips: leftover lipstick that won't come off the day after.

little black dress: an essential wardrobe item.

low drag: anything that's not high drag.

Mary, Margot, Sister, Girlah: terms of endearment. Can be applied to any queen.

Myrna fish drag: trying to look like a real woman.

Mz. Flashback: the elected head of Flashback's drag stage for a year.

new guard: the queens who want the crowns.

off the street: resigning from hooking. (Notice it's not called "going straight".)

old guard: the queens who have the crowns.

one-size-fits-all: an evil lie.

paint: to apply makeup

panstick: roll-out pancake base.

pop a tuck: a good luck wish

Some Edmonton Queens (8)

Excretia

Gretchen

DARRIN HAGEN

before you go on-stage (the drag equivalent of "break a leg".)
see also: tuck

prairie fairy: a fag from Alberta, Saskatchewan or Manitoba.

Princess: a title given by the Empress to the queen she wants for her second in command. (Usually her best friend.)

Purple City: age-old Big Onion party ritual (even straight people do this one). Hang out at the Legislature, stare into the floodlights, and then look at the skyline. Everything appears purple. No one is sure how this originated, but everybody's done it.

raccoon eyes: leftover mascara that won't come off the day after.

the Razzberries: Mrs. K., Lindee Star and Ginger Snot

Reverend Bob: the ex-minister who worked the front door.

rhinestone turkey baster: a fabulous stage microphone.

screaming section: wherever Lulu and I would sit in a late-night restaurant.

smell her: see fish

the Strip: where the hookers (not all of them real women) work.

tough drag: full glamour drag, but with full facial hair, or hairy chest in a strapless gown. The day after the ball, all the men with elected boy titles have to do tough drag. Officially, it's so they can feel what it's like to be in drag all the time, but really it's just for us girls to laugh at them for a change.

tranny: originally a term for transsexuals, it eventually became an all-encompassing word for any queen.

transgender: anyone who is anywhere along the scale between man and woman, and is considering or has had surgery to correct the error.

tuck: the process of hiding the penis in a skimpy outfit.

tundra Fairy: a fag from Canada's North.

Underground: the gay scene.

Value Village: where a thrifty queen shops. Used dresses, antique costume jewelry, and platform shoes at rock bottom prices.

wicked web: the web of nylon between the cotton gusset in the crotch of your pantyhose and your actual crotch. Usually only a concern for tall queens.

work the room: mingle loudly.

The Life And Times Of Canada's Wildest Party Children:
The Edmonton Queens

The Official Crowned Heads Of The Big Onion
The First Of Houses Under Millicent
THE FIRST IMPERIAL HOUSE OF MILLICENT
Empress I Millicent
Imperial Princess I Felicia
THE SECOND IMPERIAL HOUSE OF MILLICENT
Empress II Chatty Cathy Jackson / Emperor II John
Imperial Princess II Hoopie
THE THIRD IMPERIAL HOUSE OF MILLICENT
Empress III Nikki / Emperor III Tony
THE FOURTH IMPERIAL HOUSE OF MILLICENT
Empress IV Rayette / Emperor IV Michael
The Fifth Imperial House Of The Undersea World Of Atlantis
Empress V Trixie / Emperor V Joeboy
The Sixth Imperial House Of Polaris: The Star Court
Empress VI Lindee Star / Emperor VI Mr. Vera
Imperial Princess VI Mrs. K.
The Seventh Imperial House Of The Megamentals
Empress VII Mrs. K. / Emperor VII Sam
Imperial Princess VII Lexy Con/Trash
The Eighth Imperial House Of The Crazy 8's
Empress VIII Mary Mess / Emperor VIII Rick
Imperial Princess VIII Lulu LaRude
The Ninth Imperial House Of The Dirty Diamonds
Empress IX Lulu LaRude / Emperor IX Buster Box
Imperial Princess IX Gloria Hole
The Unified Decade Imperial House Of
Divine Excellence And Motherly Love
Empress X Amii L. Nitrate (abdicated) / Emperor X Mr. X
Empress Regent Mother Jean
Imperial Princess X Tina
The Eleventh Imperial House Of Age And Adventure
Empress XI Beverly Crest / Emperor XI Sig
Imperial Princess XI Ora Fice
The Twelfth Imperial House Of
Vicious Knights And Imperial Pleasures
Empress XII Ora Fice / Emperor XII Teddy Bear
Imperial Princess XII Mandy Kamp
The Thirteenth Imperial House Of Poodles And Pitbulls
Empress XIII Gracie Spoon / Emperor XIII Jim
Imperial Princess XIII Brandy

The Fourteenth Imperial House Of Silver Tongs And Dance
Empress XIV Leah Weigh / Emperor XIV Rob
Imperial Princess XIV Twiggy
The Most Excellent Fifteenth House Of The Divining Rod...
A New Decade
Empress XV Twiggy / Emperor XV Pierre
Imperial Princess XV Jackie
The Sixteenth Imperial House Of Women On The Edge:
The Northern Light Star Court
Empress XVI Mandy Kamp / Emperor XVI Brian
Imperial Princess XVI Ginger Snapped
The Recycled Environmentally Friendly
Seventeenth House Of Androgyny
Empress XVII Mary Mess / Emperor XVII Mr. Vera
Imperial Princess XVII Marsha Black
The Eighteenth Carrot House Of Life, Liberty and Pursuit...
Empress XVIII Marsha Black / Emperor XVIII Tony Curtis
Imperial Princess XVIII Gretchen
The Nineteenth Imperial House Of G.I. Gals And Glamorous Joes
Empress XIX Gretchen Wilder / Emperor XIX Jim
Imperial Princess XIX Natasha
The Twentieth Color-Coordinated House Of
Lace, Lame And Lounge Acts
Empress XX Tootzenelda Woofenpeekhole / Emperor XX Mr. Vera
Imperial Princess XX Weena

The Official Crowned Heads Of Club Flashback
(or...Divas with a bar tab.)

1976-1991

Mz Flashback 1 Millie / Mr Flashback 1 Joey
Mz Flashback 2 Felicia / Mr Flashback 2 Bobby
Mz Flashback 3 Gino / Mr Flashback 3 Roy
Mz Flashback 4 Bianca Bang-Bang / Mr Flashback 4 Mr Vera
Mz Flashback 5 Gracie / Mr Flashback 5 Leonard
Mz Flashback 6 Tina / Mr Flashback 6 Lee
Mz Flashback 7 Trash / Mr Flashback 7 David
Mz Flashback 8 Lexy Con / Mr Flashback 8 Gerry
Mz Flashback 9 Gloria Hole / Mr Flashback 9 Mr K
Mz Flashback 10 Tallulah / Mr Flashback 10 Dorky-Louise
Mz Flashback 11 Twiggy / Mr Flashback 11 Neon
Mz Flashback 12 Kim Burly / Mr Flashback 12 Deejay
Mz Flashback 13 Cleo / Mr Flashback 13 Zola
Mz Flashback 14 Gretchen Wilder / Mr Flashback 14 Hansel
Mz Flashback 15 a) Christine 15 b) Leah Weigh
15 c) Ginger Snapped 15 d) Mandy Kamp

The Official Appointed Entertainers Of The Year

I. Chatty Cathy Jackson (1982)
II. Mrs. K. and Sam (1983)
III. Lindee Star (1984)
IV. Lulu LaRude (1985)
V. Gloria Hole (1986)
VI. Twiggy (1987)
VII. Kim Burly (1988)
VIII. Cleo (1989)
IX. Twiggy (1990)
X. Mandy Kamp (1991)
XI. Beverly Crest (1992)
XII. Kristy Krunt (1993)
XIII. Neon (1994)
XIV. The Village People (1995)
XV. Rosa Rita Refried Beans (1996)
XVI. Tootzenelda Woofenpeekhole (1997)

---

the 70s
Entertainer Of The Decade I
Chatty Cathy Jackson
*

the 80s
Entertainer Of The Decade II
Gloria Hole
*

the 90s
Entertainer Of The Decade III
Twiggy

DARRIN HAGEN

BIG SLOPPY KISSES...
Gloria broadcasts her thanks to:

- JUDY LAWRENCE & HEATHER D. SWAIN for offering me the opportunity to go solo.
- RON JENKINS for getting the best out of me, and for directing me to act like myself.
- THE EDMONTON FRINGE FESTIVAL for a decade of putting up with drag madness, and for never saying no.
- KLODYNE RODNEY for listening to every story over the phone as it came out of my pen.
- GUYS IN DISGUISE (KYLE EDGAR, LOU BAISI, KIM KNAPP, TERRIE GRIEVE, MICHAEL MCDONNELL, SHANANN KOLSKOG, JAMES ROSS, MARK WARREN, CHUCK GILLIS, CHRISTOPHER PETERSON and KEVIN HENDRICKS) for letting me talk them all into going public with their art.
- FAT CAT MEDIA RELATIONS for making me the most over-publicized queen in Fringe history.
- THE GIRLS AT CATALYST THEATRE (BRENDA O'DONNELL, JACKIE RICHARDSON, AND RUTH SMILLIE) for starting the Loud 'N Queer Cabaret (where I wrote my first queen story), and letting me explore every possible facet of Art.
- MARCIE WHITECOTTON-CARROLL for all the typing (until I learned how to do it myself).
- STANLEY CARROLL for the fabulous clothing over the years.
- DIEDRE HACKMAN AND CONCRETE CLOTHERS for the blue sequin dress in the Sun fashion shoot.

- CLIFFORD MCDOWELL for ten years of fabulous hair at a moment's notice.
- BEN HENDERSON AND THEATRE NETWORK for the holdover.
- CJSR AND GAYWIRE for the countless times they've let me read on the air.
- FIRST NIGHT FESTIVAL AND MEMI VON GAZA for the throne.
- HENK KALKMAN for the queenly valance.
- MARK BILKO for "borrowing" the dinghy for the City Hall photo shoot.
- EDMONTON CITY HALL for not throwing me out of the reflecting pool.
- IAN JACKSON for making me look like a million bucks when I felt like $1.49.
- DORKY-LOUISE for the amazing hot-glue masterpiece.
- JANICE WILLIAMSON and ROBERT W. GRAY for treating me like a writer before I knew I was one, and for the many chances to read excerpts in front of an audience.
- DICK FINKEL AND PAMELA ANTHONY for bringing drag to street level.
- MICHAEL VONN for making me realize that our stories deserved to be heard.
- ANNIE KRISHER for the assistance in getting in touch with queens I haveln't heard from in years.
- SEAN C. WAGER for the Guys in Disguise logo.
- DAVID HENNESSEY (Mr. Flashback 7) for saving me from tech hell at the 1987 Fringe, and also for the early encouragement at every step of the way.
- TREVOR ANDERSON for the lip glossary idea.
- RICK JESSOME for the inspired titles.
- CATHERINE HEDLIN for flogging the book before it was even printed.
- NEON for fifteen years of make-up, support, partnership and for putting up with the diva-to-end-all-divas.
- REBAR (ALL OF YOU) for five years of Guys in Disguise.
- BRAD COURTNEY for convincing us that Edmonton was finally ready to meet us.
- EVERYONE WHO EVER WORKED, PARTIED OR THREW UP AT FLASHBACK
- CANDAS JANE DORSEY AND TIMOTHY J. ANDERSON for the amazing opportunity they've provided me. Not many publishers would take a chance like this on a Queen like me. This experience has changed my life. Thank you for urging me to stay brave and honest while writing.
- THE EDMONTON THEATRE COMMUNITY for being the best playground in the world for discovering possibilities. Over and over, I am surprised at how generous and fertile this ground is. Thanks for the

Sterling. To every performer and director and designer I've admired in the last decade, be aware that I've stolen every idea of yours that I liked.

- MY FAMILY (MOM, DAD, TREVOR, SHAWNA, CHAD, CHRISTIAN AND GRANDMA) for allowing me to be whatever I had to be to survive. You guys are the best.
- JOHN REID for having a club called Flashback and for having a Mz. Flashback to represent it. Nothing will ever match that amazing decade for sheer excitement. All of us who were changed by that experience are better humans because of it; and the legacy lives on in all of us, in all that we do and create. Did you have any idea what you were creating when I was crowned Mz. Flashback? Accept the responsibility! This is all your fault.!
- KEVIN HENDRICKS for fifteen (is it that long already?) years of belief, faith, patience, love and understanding. None of any of this would have happened without you by my side. You're a constant reminder of the endless possibilities we've created, the losses we've survived, and the magic time when we first met. Not many men would have put up with Gloria's antics like you did, and for that, both of us are eternally grateful. Thank you for keeping me grounded so my mind can fly. It's a gift I treasure more than you'll ever know.
- And lastly, to all the queens who gave me permission to come clean about the world we used to inhabit, thank you for allowing me to capture that time forever. I hope you cherish these experiences as much as I do. The opportunity to be back in that world for the year-and-a-half it took to write this book was a real Flashback, and for that I will always be grateful.

Oh my God, Im starting to sound like Sally Field; I'd better stop. To the potentially thousands of people I have missed in these thank-yous, my sincere apologies. The eighties have played some wicked tricks on my memory.

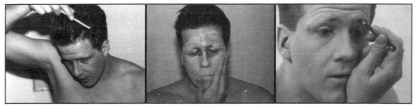

It's the same river, but older. It carries more within itself...

Photo credits

Ellie Brewer: pp. 100, 102, 104
Michael Brennan: pp. dedication page, 14, 31, 161
Perry Crann: p. 147
Anne Grant: pp. 116, 118, 123
Darrin Hagen: p. 74
Peter McClure: cover, frontespiece (the Burger Barn shots)
the Flashback collection: pp. 11,12, 21, 22, 23 36, 38, 40, 41(all), 42(top),
43, 47(both), 48, 52, 55, 58, 60(bottom), 67, 68, 71, 75(all), 76, 78, 79, 80,
82, 84, 87, 89, 90, 92, 95(all), 97(all), 103, 109, 112, 115(all), 121, 127,
135(middle, bottom), 146, 154, 155(top), 156(both)
Ian Jackson: pp. 45, 136, 151
the Rick Jessome collection: p. 51
the Lulu collection: p. 62
Scott Melnyk: p. 135(top)
Celine Nadon: p. 142
the Neon collection: pp. 18, 28, 30, 132
Ivan Seymour: (artist) p. 25(both)
Richard Siemens: pp. 106, 111, 114
David Williams: p. 60 (top)
Unknown: pp. 8, 20, 26, 34, 42(bottom), 56, 64, 80, 93, 124, 126, 129,
145(both), 153, 155(bottom), 163(all)

There's something special about the first time...

The Edmonton Queen: not a riverboat story was first performed
August 16,1996, at the Anniversary Stage, Arts Barns (old Bus
Barns), Fringe Theatre Festival, Edmonton, Alberta, Canada. Starring
Darrin Hagen as Gloria/himself and Mandy (Mark Warren) as the
Visual Aide. Director: Ron Jenkins; stage manager: Neon (Terrie
Grieve). Produced by Guys in Disguise (Darrin Hagen and Kevin
Hendricks). Design by Dorky-Louise (Darcy Greenough). Costumes
and lighting as required. Sound design by Darrin Hagen. During the
run, my mom coincidentally sat at the same table as my soon-to-
be publisher, who approached me after the show with the idea for
this book. I'm not saying that the two are connected, mind you...

Editor's Afterword by Candas Jane Dorsey

I am one generation further removed from the Alberta heartland than Darrin Hagen. My mother and father both grew up near Hagen's Rocky Mountain House birthplace; I was born many hundreds of miles down the river which runs through our lives, but through family reunions and an innate sense of weather, I remain linked to the source. I understand, in a very important and non-verbal way, where he comes from.

One Hallowe'en I dressed as a drag queen–a woman dressing as a man who dresses as a woman–to go to Flashback (where, had I but known it, Darrin was that night's feature performer). My friend Grace (not Gracie, the queen in this book, but the *other* drag queen of that name in Edmonton) lent me the wig and did my face. I was a black-leather-jacket-clad bundle of Attitude (something a nice prairie girl usually is not allowed to have) and people quailed from my unsmiling and patrician glare. I met people there I'd known for years, none of whom recognised Chip (named after the one on my alter-ego's shoulder). I had my ass grabbed by a man who muttered an apologetic "I'm sorry, I thought you were a sister..." when he found more there than a drag queen should have. In those few hours I enjoyed the seductive nature of–the power of–identity collapse, reversal and upset.

Darrin Hagen/Gloria Hole has lived his/her adult life in that landscape. Darrin is tall, muscular, the epitome of tanned cowboy: Gloria is a tall, beautiful dame (there is *nothing* like *this* dame!) who makes heads turn. In some ways they are opposites yet they are the same person.

Identity is, as every drag queen knows, a matter of accessorising. Gender is the set of accessories, the social construct, on which we agree to run a divided, dualised society: divided between men and women, heterosexuals and non-heterosexuals, fashion plates and fashion problems. To change the way we accessorise, to change our gender construct, is a radical act. It's far more radical, and more disturbing to the status quo, than who we sleep with. It challenges who we have *chosen* to be, or been programmed to be, rather than commenting on who we are.

Sitting in the old Bus Barns, now converted to a theatre, on August 24, 1996, watching Darrin Hagen perform *The Edmonton Queen: not a riverboat story*, I was aware that I was seeing and hearing not just an autobiographical memoir of one queen's war against mediocrity but a social history. I also recognised, with that special thrill a publisher gets, that this could be *A Book*: a book which would make an important contribution to the understanding of drag and gender rôles. Here, almost a year later, is that book. Ladies and Gentlemen–and do you know which is which?–I commend to you, my friend and fellow writer, the Edmonton Queen.

Tired of the status quo? Sick of the same old bedtime reading?
Looking for a challenge?
Well, look no further.

The Word is Out: SLIPSTREAM GIVES GOOD BOOK!

If you liked *The Edmonton Queen*, try this:

...if you have ever felt an erotic impulse, you will find yourself here.

Neurotic Erotica
by Timothy J. Anderson

ISBN: 1-895836-18-2
$15.95

Is poetry necessarily an expression of personal truth? Or can it be a series of fictions and fantasies in search of a greater truth? In this provocative examination of human sexual behaviour, award-winning playwright Timothy J. Anderson invites readers to share a dialogue about what is normal and what is neurotic in the ways humans express their sexuality. Timothy J. Anderson is an award-winning playwright, an actor who has worked in national and international productions including *Phantom of the Opera*, a classical and opera singer, a composer, a librettist, and a published short story writer.

Foreword by Dr. Robyn Mott.
Cover art by internationally renowned Polaroid artist Evergon.
Cover design by Gerry Dotto.